THE ESSENTIAL GUIDE TO
FOOD DR

A Fun Guide to Creating Snacks, Meals, and Crafts

MARY T. BELL
AUTHOR OF *JERKY: THE COMPLETE GUIDE TO MAKING IT*

Skyhorse Publishing

This is dedicated to the hope that food drying will find a welcome place in everyone's kitchen and that every farmers' market will have at least one dried food vendor. And with heart and soul, I pray that we all embrace a variety of ways to live more sustainable lives.

10 9 8 7 6 5 4 3 2 1

Library of Congress Cataloging-in-Publication Data is available on file.

Photos by Mary T. Bell, Joe Deden, Ecopolitan, NESCO® American Harvest, istockphoto, and stock.xchng.

Print ISBN: 978-1-5107-6948-9
Ebook ISBN: 978-1-5107-6961-8

Printed in China

Thank You All

Bushels of thanks go to my husband, Joe Deden. He is a willing taste tester, photographer, consultant, fellow gardener, food preservation partner, sustainable quester, and friend.

One of my best food consultants is my mother-in-law, Adeline Deden. Although she has lost most of her sight and cannot read recipes, her memory serves her well, she has a good palate, and she can feel when the texture is just right.

My best taste testers are Hunter and Alysse, our treasured grandchildren. Alysse gleefully strips rhubarb leather off the dehydrator trays and gobbles it up and Hunter loves to sample jerky.

The quest for good food is growing as people assess the value of what they consume and the link between food and good health. Much of the credit for this shift in consciousness goes to the influential chefs who use and celebrate organic and locally grown food in their restaurants. These culinary trailblazers have modeled an ethic of stewardship, healthfulness, and creativity that has helped to promote environmental thoughtfulness and food awareness.

I am proud and grateful to live in a rural community where there is a growing appreciation for the quality of our soil, our air, and our water. Our commitment to the environment was put to the test a few years ago when the world's largest tire burning plant was scheduled to be built only a few miles upstream from our community. People rallied and, thank goodness, stopped the tire-burning project in its tracks. Since this victory, people in our community have steadily worked to embrace more sustainable ways of living.

This project was strengthened by the editorial contributions and emotional support from Mary Musielewicz, Shayla Gehrke, Nancy Martinson,

Maggie Molyneaux, and my long-time, dear friend Ray Howe. Thanks to the folks at Nesco, especially Kurt Jansen, who magically transformed our home-grown photography with his patience and healing brush. Maxxx Madcap gets credit for the illustrations. This project was initiated by and thanks to the work of Paige Cram, Abigail Gehring, Tony Lyons, and Bill Wolfsthal of Skyhorse Publishing. And I am grateful to Duane Peterson for being one of the kindest people I've ever met.

Buffalo Bird Woman

One of my mentors has been Buffalo Bird Woman. She lived a hundred years ago and was one of the last Native American women to garden in the traditional Hidatsa/Mandan manner in southwestern North Dakota. Dr. Gilbert Wilson, a University of Minnesota anthropologist, recorded her knowledge in his book *Buffalo Bird Woman's Garden*. This book provides a rare and valuable window into the past by clearly documenting specific details of how Native Americans grew, harvested, dried, stored, and cooked their food. Buffalo Bird Woman gardened in the ways of the people of the Great Plains, who farmed in the same manner for a thousand years. As a messenger of the old ways, she detailed how to build drying platforms, the best days to dry corn, beans, squash, buffalo, serviceberries, prairie turnips, and more. She cached food for two years in case the next growing season was a failure.

One of my favorite Buffalo Bird Woman stories is about her garden. "Along with the other women we would sit in the watching platform to oversee our gardens," she said. "We cared for our corn in those days as we would care for a child; for we Indian people loved our gardens, just as a mother loves her children. And we thought that our growing corn liked to hear us sing, just as children like to hear their mothers sing to them. Also, we did not want the birds to come and steal our corn."

Contents

Introduction

Food Drying with an Attitude has something for everyone: vegetarians, natural food enthusiasts, omnivores, hunters, fishermen, raw food enthusiasts, gourmet cooks, gardeners, farmers, hikers, bicyclists, and even fast food junkies. Children will learn how easy it is to make yummy fruit roll-ups and sweet, healthy treats. Dog, cat, and bird lovers will find out how to dry treats for their special friends. For those with a creative flair, a dehydrator is a fabulous tool offering limitless artistic opportunities.

This book is the culmination of more than thirty years of drying food. Within these pages you will find a wide variety of recipes, along with straightforward and practical techniques and instructions.

You'll learn how to:

- Make great jerky, a wildly popular, low-fat, high-protein fast food.
- Save money and promote good health by drying fresh, frozen, or canned fruits and vegetables—from apples to watermelon, asparagus to zucchini.
- Dry locally grown, in-season, chemical-free, and preservative-free food.
- Dry fruit and vegetable purées, from applesauce to thick liquids such as spaghetti sauce and soup.
- Make exotic and nutritious raw foods.
- Prepare lightweight, portable dried foods to take along when adventuring in the great outdoors.
- Cook and bake with dried foods.

- Make terrific dried food powders.
- Dry herbs and flowers.
- Treat your pet with homemade goodies.
- Make great gifts and home decorations.

For over three decades I have promoted food drying throughout North and Central America. My husband and I live at Eagle Bluff Environmental Center in rural Lanesboro, Minnesota. Our constant goal is to do our best to minimize the demands we make on this planet and to live thoughtful, respectful, and sustainable lives.

We use our food dehydrators throughout the year. My husband hunts, so each fall we butcher deer and make lots of jerky. During the winter we

buy overripe bananas from our local grocer and dry them instead of baking cookies. In spring we pick and dry watercress from a cold stream to use in salads throughout the year. We dry asparagus and hunt for morel mushrooms. Then our gardening cycle begins with raking, tilling, and planting. After tending and harvesting, we dry, can, and freeze the bounty and sell our excess at the farmers' market. I have more than a hundred rhubarb plants from which I make a dried rhubarb sauce called "Rhubarb Lace" that sells like hot cakes at market. All year long we use the food we dry as snacks and in cooking and baking. My husband and I value spending time in the kitchen together and we enjoy feeding our family and friends good food.

My food drying passion goes back to the 1970s. I was a single parent raising two small children and putting myself through college. I had rented a house in the country and much to my surprise, when spring came I found that my side yard had once been a garden. I knew that gardening was a way to provide good food for my kids and to save money, so I rented a garden tiller, hauled and spread well-aged manure, and started planting.

In that rich soil I planted dozens of tomatoes, peppers, salad greens, and an entire package of zucchini seeds. The harvest overwhelmed me. I bought a used freezer, tried canning, experimented with oven drying, and finally built my first outdoor food dehydrator. Then, fortunately, an entrepreneurial friend gave me one of the first electric dehydrators to hit the U.S. market.

From the beginning I was fascinated with everything I dried. It was fun. It was play. My kids loved the dried food. Throughout my experimenting I kept asking, "What if?" What if I dried a tomato, what would it look like? If I added water back would it taste like a tomato? If I dried zucchini, what would it taste like?

My experimentation led me to demonstrate and sell dehydrators at an appliance store in Madison, Wisconsin. I'd set up my table, fill my dehydrator, and offer passersby samples of dried bananas, apples, applesauce, and pineapple in hopes they'd want to purchase a dehydrator. Adults would politely say they were full, or it was Lent, or they simply didn't like fruit. It was the children who relished my samples. Again and again they returned, showed me the palms of their hands, and asked for more dried fruit. Those little hands gave me the encouragement and resolve that food drying was something important. I knew that some day those little hands would grow into big hands that would have control of their wallets and be able to buy dehydrators. I trusted that these willing young people would remember how good my samples tasted. I believed it was only a matter of time and my tenacity.

As my dedication to promoting food drying grew, I had the opportunity to travel to Central America to share what I had learned. Everywhere I traveled, people seemed intrigued by and interested in my information. One day, after teaching a class in the remote village of Pearl Lagoon, Nicaragua, a man stood up and said, "Mary Bell, I want to thank you for coming all this way. I did not know that I could dry all those foods you mentioned." At that moment I knew what my trip was really about. I was encouraging people to open their minds to do something they had not thought of before. I was promoting creativity and experimentation—and that felt great!

Writing this book is about sharing what I've learned, and my intention is to give encouragement and support to others. My need to share led to my writing *Dehydration Made Simple*, which came out in 1980. In 1994 *Mary Bell's Complete Dehydrator Cookbook* was published. I published *Just Jerky* in 1996 and *Jerky People* in 2002. Here I have compiled into one book the most concise and helpful information I have gleaned through all these years of pursuing my passion—food drying.

This book presents a "can-do" attitude. I believe that you, regardless of your lifestyle and food choices, will enjoy many benefits by including food drying in your life-skills tool chest.

Getting Ready

You can do this! Drying food is easy. And fun! Even exciting! Food drying is a playful, hands-on activity that will stimulate your curiosity as well as your taste buds.

Dry fruits, vegetables, meats, fish, herbs, flowers, yogurt, pickles, sauerkraut, and even blue cheese. Make jerky and homemade fruit roll-ups. There are only two foods that you should not dry: uncooked eggs and oil. Don't try to dry oil because it just won't dry. And do not dry whole raw eggs, because drying can produce a toxic product, so just don't do it. You can dry cooked eggs, but not raw.

Never again feel guilty when it's time to clean out your refrigerator. Instead of tossing out limp celery, half an onion or a hunk of pepper—dry them!

Use a blender to grind dried celery to a powder. Then instead of buying commercial celery salt (which is mainly salt), use your 100 percent celery powder. I guarantee it will taste better than any you can purchase. After squeezing a lemon to make lemonade, cut the rind into small pieces and dry it, then when you want lemon peel, instead of buying the commercial stuff, use your own.

Simply by removing water from food you can save money, eat better, reduce waste, minimize crop loss, help stabilize the world's food supply, utilize locally grown food, and have a reliable supply of food from one harvest to the next. Food drying is revolutionary.

Have you ever bitten into a fresh peach and found it woody? Instead of adding it to the compost pile, you can dry it. When you eat the dried peach slices, you will never know that the peach wasn't juicy before it was dried. The dried peach slices will taste sweet and be full of flavor.

Not Perfect?

I realize that some people in the food world would argue that only the freshest, most pristine, blemish-free produce should ever be consumed. But one of the most interesting things I've discovered over the years is that some old, imperfect food actually dries really well. For example, I've dried a lot of apples—new apples, old apples, wrinkled apples, tart apples, and sweet apples. What has surprised me is how well old apples dry. They have a wonderful crispness and taste sweeter than before they were dried. Trust me, you cannot tell they were old once they're dried. This thrills me, because wastefulness has always bothered me. As an environmentally aware person, I appreciate the old adage "Waste not, want not." Of course, food that is spoiled, is of poor quality, or has inedible spots should not be dried.

When you go grocery shopping and find great buys, drying will provide a way to take advantage of good deals. One time I bought twelve ripe kiwis for a dollar, and we snacked on sweet, yet tart, dried kiwi slices for months.

Gardeners, next time you're tempted to search for an unlocked car to unload your excess bounty, get out your food dehydrator instead. Be adventurous and dry everything. Slice a tomato, put it on a dehydrator tray, turn the dehydrator on, then every hour or so look at it and when it feels dry, take it off the dehydrator. When you are invited to a party, take along a bowl of dried tomato chips and some dip to share with your friends.

Drying As a Preservation Method

Drying is easier and cheaper than freezing or canning. Also, it requires less energy consumption and is less nutritionally damaging. Most foods are dried fresh, although some foods are blanched before drying, which impacts water-soluble vitamins. Vitamin C is an air-soluble nutrient and can be lost in the dry air process when cells are cut and exposed to air. Fiber, carbohydrates, and minerals do not change as a result of drying. The caloric value of dried food is exactly the same as when the food was fresh. Any food that contains sugar will taste sweeter after it's dried because removing water concentrates the natural sugars.

Most of the research on food drying has been conducted on foods prepared by the commercial drying industry. There has been very little research on foods dried by the average person. It only stands to reason that fresh, locally grown food has more food value than food that is picked before it is ripe and is shipped over long distances. In addition, drying your own food will give you control over the use of additives and preservatives.

Frozen foods require a constant flow of electricity. Each month you pay money to keep water in food frozen. Then when the frozen food is thawed, it is not the same as when it was fresh because the freezing process ruptures food cells. In contrast, food drying does not cost money each month, nor is it vulnerable to power outages, and dried food does not suffer from freezer burn.

Twenty tomatoes, three different ways.

Canning is time consuming, cumbersome, and expensive. The entire process uses a lot of energy. With canning you store food in water after boiling it to destroy all the bacteria. The seal must remain airtight to keep the vacuum intact and prevent contamination. Drying doesn't require special containers or new seals and lids: recycled canning jars, lids, and seals do the trick. Canning and freezing need more storage space than dried food. When canning, we generally put about five tomatoes in a one-quart jar. In contrast, when drying tomatoes, I can put the dried slices of as many as twenty tomatoes in a one-quart canning jar or store the same amount in a one-quart self-sealing plastic bag.

Drying is less work. It doesn't take a huge commitment of time. With canning you must finish what you start, and you need a sizeable supply of food in order to begin. With food drying you can dry a little food at one time and the dehydrator does the work—not you.

Nutritional Study *Dr. Dorothy Pringle, a University of Wisconsin professor of nutrition, evaluated the diets of the residents of the village of Puerto Cabezas, Nicaragua. From February through July, the people had a diet rich in vitamin A, but from August to January they suffered from vitamin A deficiency. This cycle corresponded to the mango crop that began to ripen in February and continued to be harvested through July.*

Emergency Readiness

Our grandparents and many of our parents, whether rich or poor, thought ahead to what they'd eat next week, next month, even next year. Historically, food drying and storage were commonplace and considered wise. Foresight and survival were synonymous.

Implementing a home food storage program has always been and will always be a good idea. Being prepared can help us through all kinds of emergencies, whether it is a harvest loss, a disruption in the fossil fuel supply, or the consequences of climate change.

The True Cost of Food

In my opinion, the true cost of food is more than what you pay at the store. The true price should factor in where and how the food is grown and the energy and transportation costs of getting it to the consumer. It is estimated that food travels about 1,500 miles before it reaches our kitchens. Consider that most of the weight of food (80 to 90 percent) is water. Water weighs eight pounds a gallon. Wouldn't it be a good idea to dry food where it is grown and transport it without water? Wouldn't that be cheaper than dragging water across continents? Reducing weight reduces both packaging and storage space.

Fresh foods are perishable and drying can help eliminate waste on both a personal and a commercial level. For example, one year we planted two hundred tomato plants. I dried and packaged all the extra tomatoes and stored them in plastic bags in the freezer. In spring I took my dried tomatoes to market before any tomatoes were on the vine. We sold out before the next tomato crop was ready. Our tomatoes weren't wasted and I put some money in the bank.

Similarly, growers could profit by drying any excess produce and gradually releasing dried foods into the marketplace. This approach could help to moderate the plunge in prices that results when a crop is harvested all at one time.

Shouldn't the true cost of food include the environmental impact of putting chemicals in our soil, air, water, and ultimately our bodies? Isn't it time we consider our responsibility to the global community?

Vitamin A deficiency hinders growth and development and lowers resistance to infections. Vitamin A is retained during the drying process. Dried mangoes stored in airtight containers and kept out of light have a six-month shelf life. One solution to cyclic vitamin A deficiency is to eat fresh mangoes for six months and the rest of the year eat dried mangoes.

Why it's important never to throw away bananas!

I'll never forget the shock my husband and I had when we toured a banana plantation in Belize. Mountains of bananas twenty feet high and twenty feet wide lined both sides of the road as we drove into the plantation. Our

guide told us, "These 'reject bananas' are not up to buyers' standards." Although edible, they were "not perfect enough" for the United States market. Adding to this waste was the environmental degradation caused by growing bananas. "The coral reef bordering the plantation is dying," our guide said sadly. He blamed the demise of the precious coral reef on the fertilizer and pesticide run-off from the frequent spraying of the banana crop.

If consumers actually paid the real cost of growing, harvesting, and transporting bananas, the cost should include cleaning up and restoring environmental damage. Banana growers could make more money by setting up a drying operation instead of wasting a substantial portion of their crop. Imperfect reject bananas can become deliciously sweet, dried chips without added sugar or preservatives. When you find on-sale brown-spotted bananas, buy them, take them home, dry them, and have nutritious snacks as you drive to work, fly on a plane, trek over a mountain, or put a snack in your kids' lunch bags.

A Bigger Vision

After all these years thinking about drying food and planting and harvesting, I believe that the single most important thing each one of us can do to balance the world's food supply is to take more responsibility for securing our own food. By utilizing locally grown food, we can be more independent and self-sufficient. Each one of us can strive to minimize our impact on this planet. Grow food yourself or support those who sell at your local market. Money spent locally strengthens your community.

> Food is our most intimate connection to the land. It is our source of health and vitality and the centerpiece of family, ethnic, and community traditions. It reflects who we are and what we value.

Drying food helps promote a simpler, sustainable, and more self-sufficient lifestyle. I believe that if each one of us would take more opportunities to obtain and preserve a reliable supply of locally grown food, we could change the world. We would eat better, save money, reduce waste, and be involved in meaningful, creative, nurturing, and environmentally sustainable activities.

Food drying could alleviate the imbalance in the world's food supply and mitigate starvation and suffering. I believe that the distribution of resources is the underlying cause of much of the world's turmoil. I wonder, should we be so confident that war and starvation always happen "over there"? When something happens to one of us, it happens to us all, and, one way or another, the impact is felt.

Drying Over Time

Growing, harvesting, and preparing food has directed the course of history and changed life on earth. Drying food is part of our human history. Hunters and gatherers learned about caching and preserving food from watching big cats drag their prey up into trees where it hung, safe from critter competition, and dried in the sun and wind.

There is no limit to human creativity. On hot, windy days, Native Americans dried corn, squash, beans, and meat on drying platforms. Incas dried potatoes in the dry mountain air. Nuts were placed in coarsely woven sacks, onions were braided, and herbs were bundled together and hung up to dry. Food has been dried on sun-warmed rocks, on racks placed above wood

> *The ultimate solar collector would focus the sun's heat and have a system that tracks the sun. It would also have vents to control the temperature, a back-up heat system, and a way to channel the wind.*

fires, and on rooftops. Windowsills, stovetops, and gas, electric, microwave, and convection ovens have been used to dry food. Food to be dried has been placed on cookie sheets or cooling racks set near heat registers, on radiators, near exhausting warm refrigerator air, and even in car windows.

> *Solar drying is a great idea. It has the potential to be energy efficient, universally available, and an environmentally friendly method that completes the natural cycle of the sun's heat and drying winds to remove water from food. In practice, however, it is dependent upon weather, which is unpredictable, and can result in uneven drying and food quality. Solar drying can take several days. Each night the food has to be protected to prevent dew from collecting. To successfully dry food outside you need low humidity, full sun, and lots of wind.*

Getting Set

Food drying is the oldest method of preserving food, but now, for many people it is a new venture.

My first choice of method for drying food is to use a good food dehydrator. With the option of electricity, drying food is easier, you get consistent results, and the process is more reliable.

One of the most important things to remember is to keep your dehydrator where it is easily accessible. Frequency of use can simply boil down to having it handy. If your dehy-drator is set conveniently on the counter and you come in from the garden with too much zucchini, or you've bought too many tomatoes at the farmers' market, or you've checked your refrig-erator and found an apple you know you won't eat, you can easily dry these foods.

> **Tips and Good Ideas**
> - Wash hands before handling food.
> - Read through recipes and directions completely before you begin trying something new.
> - Make sure you have the ingredients and utensils you will need before starting a recipe.
> - Dripping and spilling are okay.
> - Think creatively.
> - Feel free to substitute ingredients.
> - Consider the finished product a work of art.
> - Wonder where and how food is grown.

About Dehydrators

Electric dehydrators are simple kitchen appliances that heat and dry air to draw water out of food. A good food dehydrator has both a temperature control and a fan. Food is placed on the dehydrator trays, the dehydrator is turned on, the temperature is set, and within hours the food is dry.

Electric dehydrators work in any weather, on rainy and high humidity days, and during the night. Drying food inside your home means you do not have to deal with dust, bugs, or hungry birds. Electric dehydrators are consistently reliable and eliminate the guesswork of drying food in the sun, in the oven, or over a smoky fire.

A dehydrator needs a fan to force dry air through food and remove water. Dehydrators that do not have a fan require tray rotation in order

for dry air to reach all the food. Tray rotation takes time and attention. In other words, you may need to set your alarm clock, get out of bed, and go to the kitchen in the middle of the night to juggle trays. Trust me— dehydrators that require no special attention get more use.

Electric food dehydrators vary in size, style, and design and range in price from $30 to $300. Some dehydrators are round, with a base, a lid, and trays that are stacked one on top of another. For round dehydrators, the heat source and fan are either on the bottom or on the top, and are connected by the stacking trays. Dry air flows vertically through the trays and across each tray. You can also find square and rectangular dehydrators, which are cabinets that look like microwave ovens. They generally have removable trays and a front door. The cabinet style dehydrator has a heating element and fan mounted on the back, which sends dry air throughout the drying chamber.

> **Keep in Mind**
> - All fruits dry best between 130 to 140 degrees.
> - Whenever possible, dry food at night when the demand for electricity is less.
> - Make it easy on yourself—dry fruit on mesh-lined dehydrator trays.

Round stackable dehydrators give you the advantage of determining the number of trays to use. Using only the number of trays you need to dry a small or large quantity of food makes your dehydrator an energy efficient appliance.

> *Dehydrators with variable thermostats have temperatures that range from 90 to 165 degrees. Some dehydrators have a preset permanent temperature of somewhere between 130 and 150 degrees.*

Dehydrator Accessories

Dehydrator trays have holes in them that allow air to flow in and around the drying food. If these holes are too large, small pieces and liquids fall or drip through.

There are two accessory sheets you can use with a dehydrator that will make drying easier and more versatile. I guarantee that you will get the most out of a dehydrator that has mesh and leather sheets. Most of the time you'll use one or the other of these sheets on a dehydrator tray before putting food on it.

I call the netted plastic sheet that has small holes in it a "mesh sheet." These handy sheets:

- Prevent foods with high sugar content, such as bananas, tomatoes, and watermelon, from sticking to the drying trays. Without a mesh sheet, sticky foods are difficult and frustrating to peel or scrape off the dehydrator tray.
- Make cleanup easier.
- Help prevent small pieces of food, like herbs, from falling through the trays.
- Minimize liquid or juice dripping down from one tray onto another.

The other accessory is a solid, food-grade plastic liner tray or sheet that fits inside a dehydrator tray and is often called a fruit roll-up or "leather sheet." Depending on the type and size of a leather sheet, it can hold one to several cups of food.

The solid liner tray provides a way to make crackers and to dry thick or puréed foods, such as applesauce, spaghetti sauce, yogurt, soups, stew, refried beans, ketchup, and pea soup.

> NOTE *If you put food on a dehydrator tray and you forget to put a mesh sheet down on the tray, there is a way to remove the stuck dried food from the dehydrator tray. Put the tray in the freezer for at least one hour. Remove the tray from the freezer and immediately, while the dried food is cold, use your fingers to push from underneath to pop the food off the tray.*

Use Leather and Mesh Together

When you put a mesh sheet on top of a leather sheet, it is easier to dry any food that contains oil. The oil drips down and collects on the leather sheet, which makes cleanup much easier. This works well when drying cooked hamburger, bacon pieces, salmon, and cheese.

Storage Containers

Dried foods must be stored in clean, moisture-proof, and airtight containers. Just as humid air turns crisp potato chips limp, dried foods can absorb moisture and gradually deteriorate if not kept in airtight containers. My first choice is to use recycled canning jars because the seal can be made tight and you can see what's in the jar. In addition, canning jars, rings, and lids can be used again and again. Stored dried food should keep for approximately one year—from one growing season to the next. Keep jars handy in your cupboard or pantry.

Dried food packaged in plastic bags and stored in the refrigerator or freezer can last decades. Dried foods take only a fraction of the space needed for fresh, canned, or frozen foods. For short-term storage, such as on a camping trip, it is acceptable to keep dried foods in self-sealing plastic bags, but for the long term, consider the refrigerator or freezer.

Herbs are ready to be stored when they are dried to the crushable stage. Dried foods containing vitamin A, like carrots, are best stored in a dark place. Vitamin A is light sensitive and can be lost when exposed to light for longer than six months. As for fruit, because sugar acts as a natural preservative, very sweet fruits don't need to be dried as completely as less sweet fruits. All vegetables are dried until hard. Meat made into jerky should bend like a green willow when dry.

CANNED PINEAPPLE
PINEAPPLE FLOWERS

BANANAS

APPLES

MORE FRUITS
FRUIT AND NUT CRUNCH • CURRIED TRAIL MIX

MELONS
CAN'T A LOUPE CANDY • COLD MELON SOUP

BERRIES
STRAWBERRY MERINGUE COOKIES

RHUBARB POPCORN

PARTY TIME BRIE

Fruits

Knowing that raisins are dried grapes should help you under-stand what happens when the water has been taken out of a food. Dried foods are common in today's marketplace, with dried bananas, dates, mangos, apricots, and pineapple avail-able at most grocery stores. You will soon understand just how easy it is make your own dried fruit. It starts with buying a can of pineapple rings, some bananas with brown spots, and a jar of natural applesauce. Then follow the directions for drying bananas on page 5 and applesauce on page 22, and you will have learned the basics for drying a wide variety of fruits and vegetables.

CANNED PINEAPPLE

A weighty idea: With a scale, weigh fresh food before drying and weigh it again after it's dry. This will help you to become familiar with the amount of water eliminated during the drying process. | Once dried, an entire 20-ounce can of pineapple rings will weigh 4 ounces and fit in the palm of your hand.

1. Open a can of pineapple rings. 2. Pour into a colander and drain away the juice. 3. Place a dehydrator tray on your counter and put a mesh sheet inside the dehydrator tray. 4. Lay the pineapple rings on the mesh-lined dehydrator tray without overlapping any rings. 5. Place the filled tray in the dehydrator. 6. Dry between 110 degrees and 135 degrees. It will be considered "raw" if dried at 110 degrees.

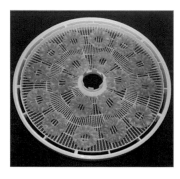

To determine when the pineapple rings are dry, every two hours turn the dehydrator off, allow a few minutes for the rings to cool, and manually check the pineapple. Warm food always feels softer than when it cools. Touching the pineapple is the best way to determine dryness—you can feel moisture in food. Each time take out a ring, eat it, and let the rest continue to dry. This helps you become comfortable with the drying process—plus the rings taste good.

Pineapple rings are dry when they bend and you do not feel any juice. They will be a little darker in color than when fresh out of the can. Fruits that have a lot of sugar do not need to be dried until hard because sugar acts as a natural preservative. How long it will take for the pineapple rings to dry will depend on the dehydrator you have, but generally it will take about eight hours when you dry at 135 degrees. Once the pineapple is dry, eat one more ring and save the rest in an airtight storage container.

Other Canned Fruits

Now that you've dried canned pineapple, try other canned fruits, like maraschino cherries, peaches, and mandarin oranges. If the canned food pieces are thicker than half an inch, slice them into ½- to ¼-inch slices; the thicker the pieces are, the longer it takes them to dry.

Dry a Fresh Pineapple

Choose a fresh, yellow-golden, sweet-smelling pineapple. To select a good pineapple, pull a leaf from inside the cluster. It should release easily and will feel slightly moist.

Cut the pineapple in half the long way. Cut each half into three equal boat-shaped pieces. Turn each piece on its side and cut out the core. Cut slices into ½-inch thick pieces, then dry. For a raw food, dry at 110 degrees and up to 135 degrees for regular drying.

Quality Time *Drying food is a great way for adults and children to spend quality time together. Once children are shown how easy it is to dry food, they'll be able to make their own snacks. A dehydrator is safer than a stove or an oven because most drying is accomplished between 100 and 135 degrees.*

Red Pineapples *Dry pineapple rings only halfway and then remove from the dehydrator tray. Place rings in a bowl and cover with cranberry juice. Let soak 15 minutes. Drain the red pineapple rings and return to the dehydrator until drying is complete. Red pineapples are festive and delicious and will have all your friends wondering where you found such an unusual fruit!*

PINEAPPLE FLOWERS

Fancy dried fruit is an attention-getter as a garnish for baked goodies.

• 1 fresh pineapple • 20 dried round strawberry slices • 1 tablespoon honey

Cut the top and bottom off the pineapple. Use a knife to cut all the skin off and trim the sides to make it round. Then cut ¼-inch "V-shapes" in the sides of the pineapple every inch and continue making V-cuts around the entire pineapple. With an electric slicer, cut the pineapple in ⅛-inch rounds.

Lay the pineapple rounds on a mesh-lined dehydrator tray. Dry 1 hour at 135 degrees. Within this time the pineapple should become pliable.

Remove a pineapple slice from the tray and place it over the rounded side of a lightly oiled tablespoon. This is how you get the pineapple to lift so it has a rounded shape and looks more like a flower petal. Try to get as much lift as possible from at least half of the pineapple slices. Place the tablespoon with the pineapple on it back on the dehydrator tray. Continue drying until the slices are dry, yet not too hard.

Remove spoon. Remove slices from tray and flex them to form flower shapes. Put two slices together to make a flower. Place a drop of honey on the center of the bottom slice and press the two pineapple slices together. Put another drop of honey in the center of the top slice and place a small round slice of dried strawberry or several dried grapes in the pineapple's center.

BANANAS

Choose bananas that have brown spots on the skin. Brown spots tell you the natural sugars have developed, so when the banana chips are dry they will taste sweeter. | Interestingly, the darker the banana's skin, the lighter the dried banana chips.

Peel and cut away any bruised or damaged areas on the banana.

Slice the banana into ¼-inch rounds.

Count the slices you get from one banana.

One average-sized banana yields about 20 ¼-inch banana slices.

Place a mesh sheet on the dehydrator tray to prevent banana slices from sticking to the tray.

Lay the banana slices on the mesh-lined tray without overlapping.

For a raw food, dry at 110 degrees and up to 135 degrees for regular drying. Banana chips generally dry in 8 to 12 hours at 135 degrees.

To check for dryness, take a banana chip off the dehydrator tray and let it cool. Dried banana slices are chewy and a little sticky, with a caramel-like color. Banana slices do not have to be dried until they are hard because the natural sugars act as a preservative. The drying time will vary depending on the type of dehydrator, the temperature used, piece size, sugar content, and the number of trays on the dehydrator.

To make banana chips similar to those you buy, choose green bananas. Green bananas hold their shape and are easier to handle than soft, ripe bananas. To keep green bananas lighter in color, dip the slices in pineapple juice before drying. You can add honey to the pineapple juice, but be prepared for a sticky banana that takes longer to dry.

Colored Banana Chips • Make red, green, orange, and purple banana chips by dipping unripe green banana slices in various flavors of Jell-O. • 3-ounce package Jell-O • ½ cup warm water • 5 medium-sized green bananas, sliced into ¼-inch rounds • Mix Jell-O and water. Dip banana slices and let soak 5 minutes to absorb color. Place on a mesh-lined dehydrator tray. For a raw food, dry at 110 degrees and up to 135 degrees for regular drying.

> **NOTE** *Commercially dried bananas are different from home-dried. Commercial bananas are crisp and light in color because they are fried in coconut oil, sweetened, flavored with banana flavoring, then dried. Homemade dried bananas are just plain dried.*

APPLES

All apples are good to dry, including some old apples. | If you want a sweet dried apple, try Golden Delicious, and for a tart dried apple, try Granny Smith.

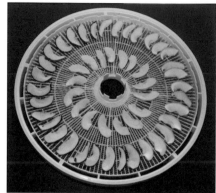

Wash apple.

Cut in half.

Remove any damaged, bruised, or bad spots.

Since peeling is a matter of choice, leave the peel on one half of the apple and peel the other half. When the apple is dry, decide which you like best—peeled or not peeled.

Cut in quarters.

Remove the core, then cut each quarter into ¼-inch slices.

Pretreatment is also a matter of choice. To enhance the flavor and to keep the apple lighter in color, dip some of the apple slices in pineapple juice. Remove slices from juice and lay flat on a mesh-lined dehydrator tray without overlapping.

Dry plain or dipped apples at 110 to 135 degrees.

Drying time is generally 12 hours. The dry slices can be crisp like a chip or leathery. When you bend the slices, you should not feel any moisture.

> **Tasty Snacks** *Once the apple slices are placed on a mesh-lined dehydrator tray, sprinkle them with a mixture of sugar and cinnamon. You can also dip apple slices in maple syrup before putting them on mesh-lined dehydrator trays.*

MORE FRUITS

Now that you've dried an apple, you have the know-how you need to dry other similar fruits, such as peaches, pears, plums, nectarines, mangos, figs, and apricots. Remember that a fresh peach or nectarine that tasted woody, once tried will taste as good as one that was dripping with juice.

Always remove cores, pits, kernels, nuts, and seeds from fruit be-

fore dehydrating. Any fruit with tough or inedible skin, like bananas, mangos, pineapples, melons, and kiwi, must be peeled.

> Creative Idea *Carefully layer colorful dried fruits in pretty jars, tie a bow, and attach a recipe. Dried apples, dried pineapple, dried cranberries, dried kiwi, and dried plums make an attractive combination.*

To Peel or Not to Peel—That Is a Question

Peeling fruits with tender, edible skin is a matter of personal preference. To find out if you prefer the taste and texture of peeled or unpeeled fruit, cut a fruit in half, peel only one half, cut both halves into ¼-inch pieces, then proceed with drying. It is important to experiment and find out what you and your family like best. Personally, I like the texture of the peel left on pears, peaches, and nectarines, but I prefer dried apples that have been peeled.

> NOTE *An apple peeler that also thinly slices the apples works extremely quickly and produces evenly sized pieces.*

Why Dip?

When you bite into an apple, then set it down on a plate for a couple of minutes, you can see that the flesh of the apple darkens in color from exposure of the inner cells to the air. This chemical change is called oxidation. To minimize darkening, you can dip foods in various antioxidant solutions before drying. Dipping solutions are antioxidants that contain vitamin C, ascorbic acid, and/or sodium bisulfate. I like to use pineapple juice with fruit, and lemon juice and salt with vegetables. Remember, dipping is a cosmetic treatment and not a requirement for drying.

> Forget the idea of sulfuring. It was common when food was dried outdoors where insects want their share of the yummy food. Sulfuring helps keep food brighter in color and acts as a preservative, but it is a lot of work and adds sulfur to food.

Dipping Directions

Put apple slices in a bowl with pineapple juice.

Stir gently with fingers to make sure all surfaces are covered.

Let soak 2 minutes. The longer the pieces soak, the more flavor is absorbed.

Remove and place on a mesh-lined dehydrator tray and dry.

> **Fun Dips** Dip apple slices in cranberry, grape, or orange juice to change the color and add flavor. Flavored liquors are a sophisticated way to add depth to fruit; try raspberry, cherry, almond, hazelnut, and amaretto.
>
> **Storing Tip** Store dried fruits—apples work well—in a jar with hardened chunks of brown sugar. The dried fruit picks up the flavor of the sugar.
>
> **After Drying** Dip one corner of a piece of dried fruit in melted white or dark chocolate. Set on wax paper and allow time to cool. Share only when forced. (Just kidding!)

FRUIT AND NUT CRUNCH

Everybody loves this fantastic concoction. It is almost a complete meal and has satisfied many a hiker, biker, and trail rider. I add beer nuts because they are salty, but any nut will do. Substitute any dried fruits that appeal to you. | Makes approximately 48 2-inch squares.

• 2 cups rolled oats • 1 14-ounce can non-fat sweetened condensed milk • 1 cup dried apples • 1 cup dried grated coconut • 1 cup dried banana slices • 1 cup dried canned peaches • 1 cup beer nuts • ½ cup dried pear slices • ½ cup dried cranberries • ½ cup raw cashew pieces • ½ cup slivered almonds

In a large bowl, mix together oats and one-third of the condensed milk. Use a knife to cut the condensed milk into the oats. Add apples and coconut and stir. Separate the banana and peach slices so they do not stick together. Add beer nuts. Stir. Add another third of the condensed milk. Stir. Separate pear slices from one another and add to mixture. Add cranberries, cashews, and almonds and stir thoroughly. Let sit one hour.

Lightly oil two leather sheets. Divide mixture evenly and spread on each sheet. To do this, I wet the palms of my hands so I can use my hands to press this sticky mixture flat on the sheets. Dry approximately 3 hours at 135 degrees or until the texture becomes similar to peanut brittle. Cool and break into 2-inch squares.

CURRIED TRAIL MIX

Increase or decrease the amount of curry depending on your taste. Try adding raisins, dried mango pieces, and chunks of dried plain yogurt. | Makes 7 cups.

• 1 cup dried Can't A Loupe Candy (see opposite page) • 1 cup pumpkin seeds • 1 cup sunflower seeds • 1 cup pine nuts, toasted • 1 cup cashews • ½ cup coconut • ½ cup dried canned pineapple, cut in ½-inch pieces • ½ cup dried peaches, cut in ½-inch pieces • ½ cup dried canned pears, cut in ½-inch pieces • 2 tablespoons curry powder

Mix all ingredients together and store in an airtight container.

MELONS

Melons have tough skins and seeds that must be discarded. To pick the right melon, push on the soft spot, then smell to detect fragrance. The melon should feel heavy for its size, should yield slightly to pressure and not be overripe. Watermelons sound hollow when thumped. Dried watermelon is very sweet. | A ½-inch piece of fresh ripe watermelon dries paper-thin.

Can't A Loupe Candy *Depending on how much you like ginger, feel free to adjust the amount used in this recipe. One tablespoon is for those who really like ginger.*

1 medium-sized cantaloupe, cut in ¾-inch cubes • ¾ cup powdered sugar • 1 tablespoon powdered ginger

Mix sugar and ginger together. Dip one side of each melon piece into the sugar mixture. Place dipped side up on a mesh-lined dehydrator tray. For a raw food, dry at 110 degrees or up to 135 degrees for regular drying.

COLD MELON SOUP

This is a treat in winter, when good melons are hard to find. | Makes 4 servings.

Put melon and broth in a saucepan and heat just until boiling. Remove from heat and add ginger and cinnamon. Stir. Cover and let cool for 15 minutes. Add butter and sugar. Place in a blender, add cream and milk, and purée until smooth. Refrigerate until cold. Add onion, stir, spoon into bowls and garnish with prosciutto or berries and mint.

- 1 cup dried honeydew melon or cantaloupe, ½-inch pieces • 2 cups chicken broth
- ¼ teaspoon ground ginger • ¼ teaspoon ground cinnamon • 2 tablespoons butter
- 1 tablespoon firmly packed brown sugar • 1 cup whipping cream • ½ cup milk
- 1 tablespoon green onion, chopped fine • ½ cup diced prosciutto, cut in ½-inch cubes, or sliced berries for garnish • 1 teaspoon crushed dried mint

BERRIES

There are two categories of berries: tender-skinned, such as strawberries; and tough-skinned, such as cranberries. The two categories are dried differently.

Discard any leaf matter, cut out the core, and slice the tender-skinned strawberries into ¼-inch thick rounds. For raspberries, check under their tender skin to make sure no bugs are hiding. Simply spread the raspberries on the

mesh-lined dehydrator trays and dry at 135 degrees until they are hard.

The second category is berries that have tough protective skins, such as blueberries, grapes, and cranberries. Their tough skin holds water inside. To dry these berries the outer skin must be broken so dry air can get inside.

To break the skin of cranberries, blueberries, or grapes:

1) Cut each berry in half with scissors or a knife, or

2) put berries in a heatproof bowl and pour boiling water over them. Berries should be submerged until their skins pop. Drain. Be careful that the berries do not sit too long in the boiling water, lose their shape, and turn into a sauce. If this happens, purée the berries and make leather.

Once the skins are broken there are various ways to sweeten the berries.

Sweeten Berries in a Sugar Solution

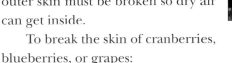

• 1 cup sugar, Karo syrup, or honey • ½ cup water • 1 12-ounce package fresh cranberries

Combine sweetener with water in a saucepan. Stir vigorously. Bring to a boil. Stir. Remove from heat. Add cranberries. Stir gently. Cover and let soak at least 4 hours. Remove the sweetened berries with a slotted spoon. Lay the sweetened berries on a mesh-lined dehydrator tray. Separate the berries so the dry air can reach as much surface area as possible and dry at 135 degrees.

NOTE *Home dried grapes look and taste different from store-bought raisins. Ripe, sweet, seedless grapes make wonderful raisins. Remember, when you get sour grapes, make raisins!*

Sweeten Berries in the Freezer

Place cranberries on a cookie sheet. Sprinkle with granulated sugar. Place in the freezer for 2 hours. Remove and arrange berries in a single layer on a mesh-lined dehydrator tray and dry at 110 to 135 degrees.

Glacé

Glacé is a sweetening process that's repeated two to four times over a period of days. It is a way to build up the sugar content in dried foods. Sugar tastes good and serves as a preservative. Fruit is submerged each day in a sweet solution, left for several hours, removed with a slotted spoon, and dried. Then the process is repeated again and again until most of the water is replaced with sweeteners. This process works best with hard fruits, such as oranges, lemons, grapefruits, citrus peels, apples, apricots, cherries, pineapple, and prunes.

- 2 cups sugar • 1 cup water • 2 cups fruit

Put sugar and water in a pan and bring to a rapid boil. Stir constantly. Remove from heat source and add fruit. Let sit a minimum of 4 hours. Remove with a slotted spoon and place on a mesh-lined dehydrator tray that has a leather sheet underneath to catch the drips. Once dry, put the fruit back in the sugar solution and repeat this process 2 to 4 times, depending on how sweet you want the finished product to be.

Make Berry Bits *One of the easiest ways to dry cranberries is by grinding fresh cranberries in a blender, then simply drying the pieces on a leather sheet.*

STRAWBERRY MERINGUE COOKIES

Use any fruit powder to make this healthy, fat-free cookie. (See page 43 for instructions on powdering dried foods.) Cover baking sheet with a cut-up brown paper grocery bag to prevent sticking. | Makes 12 cookies.

- 3 egg whites • ¼ teaspoon cream of tartar
- ¾ cup white sugar • 2 tablespoons dried strawberry powder

Preheat oven to 275 degrees. Beat egg whites and cream of tartar until foamy. Add sugar, one tablespoon at a time, and blend together. Continue beating until stiff and glossy. Do not underbeat! Once finished beating, add the strawberry powder.

Drop mounds or rounds onto the brown paper. Bake 1 hour. With small cookies, reduce the baking time so that they don't get too brown. Turn off oven. Leave meringues in oven with door closed for 2 hours. Remove from oven and finish cooling away from drafts.

RHUBARB POPCORN

I entered this recipe in the third annual Rhubarb Festival in Lanesboro, Minnesota, in 2007. The festival hosts a taste-test contest that's free and open to all festival-goers. The winner was Lynn Jacobsen and her rhubarb bars. I did not win, but this popcorn was a good way to feed the huge crowd.

- ¼ cup rhubarb lace, ground (see page 29)
- ¼ cup dried raw rhubarb, ground
- ½ cup sugar
- ¼ teaspoon salt
- 2 tablespoons butter
- ¼ cup light corn syrup
- 10 cups popped popcorn

In a small bowl, mix together rhubarb, sugar, and salt. Over medium-high heat, melt butter, stir, and add corn syrup. Stir constantly and bring to a boil. Combine the rhubarb mixture and the syrup. Pour mixture over popcorn and continue stirring until it is thoroughly coated.

To make popcorn balls, dip hands in cold water, then shape the popcorn into 2-inch diameter balls. Place on waxed paper, cool, wrap, then tie a ribbon around the ball.

PARTY TIME BRIE

This delicious party offering is also eye pleasing. Feel free to vary the ingredients, depending on what you have on hand or what colors you like best.

• 1 7- to 8-inch wheel Brie cheese • ½ cup home dried raisins • ½ cup dried canned pear pieces, cut in ½-inch pieces
• ½ cup dried canned peaches, cut in ½-inch pieces • ½ cup dried cranberries • ½ cup sunflower seeds

• ½ cup pumpkin seeds • ½ cup pine nuts, toasted • ¼ cup honey

Trim rind off Brie. Make pie-like cut lines across the top of the Brie to distinguish 6 sections and a center circle. Arrange dried fruits and nuts in each section and fill the central circle. Heat honey and drizzle over the top. Serve with crackers or bread slices.

APPLESAUCE LEATHER
VOILÁ—A POCKET SNACK • SIX FULLER POCKETS

RED, WHITE, AND BLUE PINWHEELS
GRAPE LEATHER

FRUIT AND YOGURT LEATHER

SEEDY APPLESAUCE

RHUBARB LEATHER

RHUBARB LACE

TOMATO LEATHER

FOOD CHIPS
TOMATO LEATHER CHIPS

DRAGON CRACKERS

VEGETABLE FLAX CRACKERS

PUMPKIN SEED CRACKERS

CROUTONS

RAWMELETTE

Leathers and Crackers

Children know leathers as the fruit roll-ups they get at grocery stores and health food stores. In the food drying world, dried food purées are called "leathers." And it's not just kids who love these sweet treats. Outdoor enthusiasts, gardeners, and sophisticated chefs appreciate the benefits of drying endless varieties of thick liquid combinations. These lunchbox sweets, ready-to-eat fruit snacks, and savory vegetable snacks can be rehydrated into tasty soups and sauces.

Making Leathers

Spaghetti sauce, yogurt, soups, stews, refried beans, ketchup, tomato paste, pea soup, and many other foods can be dried on solid plastic "leather" sheets that fit inside dehydrator trays. Making leathers can be as simple as drying applesauce or as sophisticated as creating fancy crackers.
I have dried blue cheese, sauerkraut, pickles, and fat-free sour cream. Although it may seem incredible, people have called me to talk about drying bee pollen and bone antlers. To top that, one guy dries and sells horse manure as plant fertilizer. (He doesn't use the same dehydrator that he uses for food).
A fellow garden club member, Sue Ommen, called. "I've got three pear trees that are full and ready for picking," she said. Immediately my husband and I loaded empty buckets and jumped into the car and drove to her home. My husband climbed the trees and picked pears until it was almost dark. Over the next week, we ate fresh pears, juice dripping down our shirts. We dried about a hundred trays of pear slices that we first dipped in pineapple juice. Then, as always, some of the pears got too ripe. I cut away the damaged and bruised parts, discarded the cores, and whipped the pears up in the blender, skin and all, and made pear leather.

The next day when my granddaughter Alysse came to visit, she devoured a whole tray of dried pear leather. Later, when we went to school to pick up Hunter, her brother, we took along a bag of pear leather. As Hunter slipped on his backpack we shared the leather with several of his friends, who kept asking for more.

Leathers are incredibly easy to make

The following tips will ensure your success:

1) Prepare leather sheets by coating them with a little oil. Oil helps to prevent purées from sticking to the leather sheets and will make it easier to peel off the finished product.

2) Leathers can be made with fresh, canned, or frozen fruits and vegetables, single food items, or in combinations. The amount of pectin in a particular fruit or vegetable can determine its ability to bond and hold together. Keep in mind that unripe fruit usually has more pectin than fully ripe fruit. Apples, apricots, blackberries, cranberries, currants, figs, grapes, peaches, and pears are good choices for fruit leathers. Cherries, citrus, melons, raspberries, and strawberries, as well as most vegetables, are low in pectin. An easy solution when making fruit leathers with these fruits and with all vegetables is to mix equal parts of high-pectin and low-pectin foods together.

3) Foods are puréed in a blender. If the food you are trying to purée is tough or becomes too thick, the blender may stall and not be able to grind all the food at one time, so begin with a little food and gradually add more. I like purées that are the consistency of applesauce.

4) Puréed raw food can darken when it's dried. To keep the dried leather light in color you can:

> Add pineapple and/or lemon juice to the purée.
> Mix a bright food, like red strawberries, beet juice, or beet powder into the purée.
> Add Kool-Aid or Jell-O for color and flavor.
> Peel food, because skins darken a purée.
> Blanch or cook food before making a purée.

5) Taste purées before drying. Remember that the dried leather will taste sweeter because the water has evaporated.

6) How long it takes a leather to dry will depend on the thickness, temperature, consistency, and sugar content of the purée. For example, a 15-inch round leather sheet that has a 2-inch hole in the center can hold up to 3 cups of purée that's spread ¼-inch thick. At a temperature of 135 degrees leathers generally dry in about 8 hours. At a temperature of 110 degrees it can take 12 or more hours. Dry leathers until they are pliable, but not tacky.

APPLESAUCE LEATHER

Applesauce is dry when it easily peels off the leather sheet without any tacky or sticky spots. This generally takes 6 to 12 hours. | The contents of a 24-ounce jar of applesauce will dry to about 3 ounces and will fit in a sandwich bag.

Open a 24-ounce jar of natural applesauce.

Spray the leather sheet with a little oil.

Place the oiled leather sheet in the dehydrator tray.

Carefully pour the applesauce on the leather sheet.

With a spatula, evenly spread the applesauce about 1/4-inch thick over the entire sheet.

Place the tray in the dehydrator.

Set the temperature at 135 degrees.

CONGRATULATIONS!!! *You have successfully dried pineapple, bananas, and applesauce. The foundation has been laid. You've graduated and are ready to dry other foods in delicious and creative ways.*

VOILÀ—A POCKET SNACK

Now let's put the dried applesauce and some dried fruits together and make a special treat. This is the ultimate pocket snack because you even eat the pocket. Just wrap the dried applesauce into a cone shape, glue with honey, tie together, and fill with dried goodies. | Makes 2 pockets.

- Scissors • Hole punch • 1 teaspoon honey • 2 24-inch long red licorice laces
- 1 sheet dried applesauce • 4 dried pineapple rings • 20 dried banana chips
- Plastic wrap • Scotch tape

Fold a sheet of dried applesauce in half and use scissors to cut it into two half circles. Wrap each half around into a cone shape. Use the hole punch to make two holes that are about an inch apart: one a ½-inch down from the top and one on the backside of the cone that you will thread the licorice through. Wrap the dried applesauce around to form a cone shape. Place 1 teaspoon honey on the inside of the applesauce flap where it overlaps and spread it with a knife. Press the two pieces together hard enough that they stick. Thread the licorice string through each hole from the inside. Pull licorice through, wrap it around to the front of the cone, and tie a bow. Fill each cone with dried

fruit and "voilà!"—you have put together what you have learned.

For a travel snack, place the filled cone facedown on a sheet of plastic wrap. Wrap tightly, tape with scotch tape, and stuff it in your pocket to take along when hiking or biking. Or put in an envelope and send it to a friend. This healthy, fat-free treat is even better when made with in-season, organic, locally grown fruit.

SIX FULLER POCKETS

In each pocket put about 10 dried apple slices, 10 dried banana slices, 10 dried pear slices, 10 dried plum slices, 5 dried pineapple slices, 4 dried kiwi slices, 6 dried strawberry slices, and ⅓ cup dried cranberries. Consider adding jerky to put a little protein in your pocket.

• 3 24-ounce jars of applesauce • 3 20-ounce cans pineapple rings (save juice for dipping) • 3 large Golden Delicious apples • 3 bananas • 4 pears • 4 plums • 12 strawberries • 3 kiwis • 12 ounces fresh cranberries • 6 24-inch-long red licorice laces • 3 teaspoons honey

Playful Treats

Try some of these fun and creative ways to flavor applesauce after it has been spread on lightly oiled leather sheets and before starting the drying process.

Valentine Applesauce
Sprinkle cinnamon and red-hot candies on the undried applesauce.

Applesauce Art

Squirt tubes of commercial frosting in wildly creative fashion (think Jackson Pollock) on the undried applesauce.

Apples and Worms

Place gummy worms in the undried applesauce.

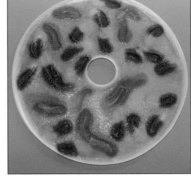

Christmas Leather

Crush peppermint candies with a rolling pin, then sprinkle on the undried applesauce.

Applesauce Cookies

Spoon a tablespoon of applesauce into little round shapes instead of making one continuous sheet. Top the applesauce with coconut, crushed nuts, or even a few M&M'S.

Twists

Dry a jar of store-bought strawberry or cherry-flavored applesauce and a sheet of plain applesauce. Wet one side of a sheet of leather. Press the two different sheets of dried fruit leather together. Cut in 1-inch strips and twist.

Caramel Apple Leather

Spread a sheet of dried applesauce out so it lays flat, then spoon softened, melted caramel on top of it. Let it cool a few minutes, roll it like a jellyroll, wrap in plastic wrap, chill, and cut in ¼-inch rounds.

Variations *Flavor purées with cinnamon, vanilla, nutmeg, extracts, chopped nuts, and herbs.*
After the purée has been spread on the leather sheet and before the drying begins, sprinkle nuts, seeds, raisins, or coconut on the purée.

RED, WHITE, AND BLUE PINWHEELS

- 1 sheet red (strawberry) leather
- 1 sheet blue (blueberry) leather
- 8-ounce package cream cheese

To get one red sheet, dry:
- 2 cups puréed strawberries
- 1 cup applesauce

To get one blue sheet, dry:
- 2 cups puréed blueberries
- 1 cup applesauce

Lay both red and blue sheets flat on a cutting board and spread the softened cream cheese on top of each sheet. Put the sheets together, roll, wrap in plastic wrap, chill, and cut. Store in the refrigerator.

Half and Half *Drying single ingredients is one way to make leathers, but by mixing various ingredients you can create amazing flavors. Apricot-apple and mango-peach leather are delicious pairings. Let your creative juices flow and experiment with endless combinations.*

1 ½ cups applesauce, raw, cooked, or canned
1 ½ cups strawberries, fresh or frozen

Purée in a blender, spread evenly on a lightly oiled leather sheet, and dry at 110 to 135 degrees.

GRAPE LEATHER

This is one of our all-time favorite leathers. When a friend offered us her dark purple grapes, we picked until our hands turned purple. We pushed the seedy grapes through a strainer and then poured the purée on lightly oiled leather sheets. We did not add anything. The leather peeled off easily and it was delicious. Dry at 110 to 135 degrees.

FRUIT AND YOGURT LEATHER

Apricot leather has been made for centuries by puréeing apricots and laying them in the sun to dry. Apricots, peaches, and pears can turn dark when dry, but adding lemon or pineapple juice helps keep a lighter color.

• 2 cups apricot purée • 1 cup plain yogurt • 1 teaspoon lemon juice • ¼ teaspoon cinnamon • ⅛ teaspoon allspice • 1 tablespoon almonds, finely chopped

Mix all ingredients together, except almonds, and spread evenly on an oiled leather sheet. Sprinkle the almonds on top. Dry at 110 to 135 degrees.

SEEDY APPLESAUCE

This treat is quite tasty and a less expensive alternative to store-bought health food bars.

- 2 tablespoons water • ¼ cup molasses
- 1 cup sesame seeds, toasted
- ½ cup date pieces • 3 tablespoons dried pears cut in ⅛-inch pieces
- 1 teaspoon black sesame seeds
- 1 teaspoon cumin • ¼ teaspoon cinnamon • 2 cups applesauce

Put water and molasses in a saucepan. Stir until warm and blended. Add the remaining ingredients. Stir well. Spread on oiled leather sheet. Dry at 110 to 135 degrees.

RHUBARB LEATHER

For over thirty years I've made rhubarb leather, but it still amazes me when I witness how much children love it. I first experienced this when hundreds of school kids devoured my rhubarb leather at a Wisconsin Historical Society event in Madison, Wisconsin. As they passed by my table, they grabbed handfuls of rhubarb leather out of big wooden bowls. It was like piranha attacking raw chicken. I tried to tell them it was rhubarb, but they were too busy or too hungry, or it was just so tasty that they failed to register what I said. I was out of rhubarb in a few minutes and was left speechless. Now I sell what I call Rhubarb Lace at our local farmers' market—and children are still my best customers!

My rhubarb leather evolved as a result of experimentation. When I first started drying rhubarb, I cut fresh rhubarb into 1-inch pieces, dried it, and later on in the season used it for sauce. It was okay, but not exciting. Then I started making rhubarb leather and found that adding a couple strawberries gave it a sweeter, more delicate taste.

RHUBARB LACE

- 3 cups fresh rhubarb, cut in 1-inch pieces
- 3 cups boiling water • ½ cup sugar
- 3 strawberries, fresh or frozen • 1 tablespoon
strawberry gelatin • ⅛ teaspoon ginger

Place rhubarb in a stainless steel pot and cover with boiling water. Let it sit at least 1 hour, until rhubarb changes color. This blanching helps eliminate some of the acidity, so less sweetener is needed. It also softens the texture, which makes it easier to purée.

Drain off water. Purée rhubarb in a blender in small batches to avoid overtaxing the blender. It may be necessary to add a little water or juice to get the rhubarb to blend. Add the remaining four ingredients and purée until smooth. Spread purée evenly on a lightly oiled leather sheet. Dry at 110 to 135 degrees. Dry until the leather peels off easily without any wet or sticky spots.

TOMATO LEATHER

Tomatoes do not have enough pectin to hold together as a dried purée, so a thickener must be added. | If you use small seedy tomatoes, strain them to get rid of the seeds.

• 2 cups tomato purée • 1 tablespoon cornstarch

Blend tomatoes and cornstarch together. In a small pan, cook over medium heat, stirring constantly until mixture thickens and reaches the consistency of applesauce. Cool and spread on oiled leather sheets to dry. Dry at 110 to 135 degrees.

Variations *Sprinkle herbs on the tomato purée before drying. Try dried basil, thyme, rosemary, and/or dried oregano and garlic powder.*

Leather Bread *Flatten raw bread dough to about ½-inch thick. Open a sheet of dried leather, dip it in water or juice, then place it on top of the dough. Sprinkle nuts, raisins, and cinnamon on top of the leather. Roll the dough up like a jellyroll, give the bread time to rise, then bake.*

FOOD CHIPS

Making food chips can be as simple as marinating slices of vegetables in a commercial salad dressing or concocting a homemade marinade. Most of the time, young, tender vegetables with vibrant colors and firm textures, like carrots, kohlrabi, peppers, rutabaga, parsnips, squash, and firm tomatoes are used to make chips, and those gigantic zucchini can also be used.

My neighbor Kitty Baker has a passion for making crackers. She has done some amazing experiments: She toasted sunflower seeds, added cooked and mashed winter squash, toasted garlic, and blended this all with fresh cilantro that she dried crisp. She toasted flaxseed, mixed it with multigrain porridge and cooked, mashed winter squash, and added raw puréed garlic. Then she sautéed sweet corn in oil, curry, and hot pepper, and then tried the same thing with thin slices of beets. She cut thin slices of squash that she soaked in a vinegar and salt solution; sprayed with flavored oil; dipped in a cilantro, mint, and ginger sauce; and then dried it until it was crisp. To top her experimenting off, she sautéed fresh snow peas, added a little curry, and dried them crisp.

Experiment with marinating vegetable slices in lemon juice, orange juice, maple syrup, salad dressings, tamari sauce, Bragg Liquid Aminos, wine, and various flavors of oil. Spice the marinade with herbs and spices, like ginger, cayenne pepper, garlic, and curry powder.

Chips dry best when they are sliced thin, dried until crisp, and stored in airtight containers. Keep them stored away from air because they easily pick up moisture.

Pumpkin or Winter Squash Leather Chips *Pumpkins and winter squash are similar. Cut each in half, remove seeds, and place in a pan with cut side down. Add a little water and bake in a 350-degree oven until soft. Remove. Cool. Scoop into a bowl, mash, and spread on lightly oiled leather sheets and dry at 110 to 135 degrees.*

FYI *A potato peeler can be used to slice the vegetables thin. Flavored dried chips are healthy snacks. Serve them with a dip instead of crackers. Crush chips into bacon-like bits and try them sprinkled on cooked pasta or on fresh salads.*

TOMATO LEATHER CHIPS

For a fun party snack, make chips out of purée combinations. Instead of making one continuous sheet, spoon little round shapes.

• 3 cups tomato purée • 2 tablespoons cornstarch • 1 tablespoon carrots, shredded
• 1 teaspoon lemon juice • ¼ teaspoon celery powder • ¼ teaspoon salt • ⅛ teaspoon dried basil • ⅛ teaspoon dried oregano

In a small pan, combine purée and cornstarch. Stir until it thickens, then add remaining ingredients. Cool and spread on oiled leather sheets and dry at 110 to 135 degrees.

DRAGON CRACKERS

When we dined at Charlie Trotter's Restaurant in Chicago, we had the most delicious crackers we've ever tasted. For months I tried to duplicate them but never got it right. So I called Charlie Trotter, and Katy from his public relations department gave me the rights to publish this recipe from his book, *Raw*. | Makes 30 crackers.

- 1 ½ cups golden flaxseed • 2 ½ cups filtered water • 2 tablespoons nama shoyu
- 2 tablespoons maple sugar • 1 ½ teaspoons chili powder • ½ teaspoon garam masala
- ½ teaspoon freshly ground cayenne pepper • ½ teaspoon minced onion
- ½ teaspoon minced garlic

Nama shoyu is an organic soy sauce made from soybeans and wheat. It is aged for four years and is made with less salt than traditional soy sauce. Garam masala is a ground mixture of cloves, cardamom, cinnamon, pepper, and nutmeg.

    Combine the flaxseed and water in a bowl and soak for 6 to 8 hours, or until the seeds absorb all the water. In a blender, combine the soaked seeds, shoyu, maple sugar, chili powder, garam masala, cayenne, onion, and garlic and process until smooth. Using an offset spatula, spread the mixture $^1/_8$-inch thick on a lightly oiled leather sheet. Dehydrate at 105 degrees for 4 hours, or until firm enough to flip the crackers onto a mesh lined dehydrator tray. Dry at 110 to 135 degrees. Once the crackers are dry, cut into 1 ½ by 3-inch pieces and continue to dry about 24 hours or until crisp. Once dry, put in an airtight container. They will last up to 2 weeks.

VEGETABLE FLAX CRACKERS

This is another version of a raw flax cracker.

- 1 cup tomato chunks • ⅓ cup red bell pepper, chopped • ⅓ cup fresh cilantro, chopped • 1 tablespoon garlic, minced • 1 tablespoon olive oil • 1 teaspoon sea salt • 1 teaspoon jalapeno, minced • 2 cups golden flaxseed

Combine everything except the flaxseed in a blender. Transfer to a bowl and add flaxseed. Stir. Spread mixture onto lightly oiled leather sheets. The thinner the mixture the more wafer-like it will dry. Dehydrate at 110 degrees for 4 hours, then transfer to a mesh sheet and dry until crisp.

PUMPKIN SEED CRACKERS

- 1 cup raw pumpkin seeds • ½ cup water
- 2 tablespoons carrots, shredded • 1 tablespoon red pepper pieces • 1 tablespoon tamari

Purée all ingredients. Add more water if necessary. Spoon on oiled leather sheets in thin rounds. When halfway dried, remove the puree from the leather sheet and put it on a mesh sheet. Then turn it over to finish drying. Dry at 110 to 135 degrees until crisp.

CROUTONS

These are the lightest croutons and they melt in your mouth.

- 5 slices French bread cut in ½-inch cubes • 1 tablespoon butter • 1 tablespoon olive oil • ¼ teaspoon salt • ¼ teaspoon pepper • ¼ teaspoon dried basil

Place bread cubes on a mesh-lined dehydrator tray, set the temperature at 130 degrees, and dry 30 minutes. Heat butter and olive oil in skillet over medium high heat and add bread cubes. Toss and coat with oil mixture. Sprinkle on salt, pepper, and basil. Return to dehydrator and dry until crisp.

Bagel Chips *Follow the same recipe as with croutons, but slice bagels very thin. For variety, dip bagel slices in orange juice. Sprinkle with garlic and dried onion or with cinnamon and brown sugar.*

RAWMELETTE

This recipe is a favorite at Ecopolitan, the Midwest's first raw food restaurant, in Minneapolis, Minnesota. This raw, no-egg omelet is a culinary masterpiece.

Shell: • 6 medium-sized ripe bananas, cut in ½-inch slices • 1 teaspoon vanilla • ½ teaspoon hazelnut extract • 2 cups coconut flakes • 1 ½ cups flaxseeds

Filling: • 1 cup macadamia nuts • 2 cups cashews • ½ cup nutritional yeast • 2 tablespoons garlic • 2 tablespoons lemon juice • 2 tablespoons apple cider vinegar • 2 jalapeno peppers, cut in small pieces • 1 ½ cup filtered water • 1 tablespoon sea salt

Topping: • fresh carrots, grated • fresh cilantro, chopped • red onions, diced • avocado slices

To make the shell, mash the bananas in a bowl, add vanilla and hazelnut extract. Blend. Mix coconut and flaxseed together. Put 1 cup of the coconut and flaxseed mixture in a blender at one time and grind. Repeat until it is all ground and powdery. Mix the flax-coconut blend with the banana mixture and 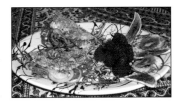 knead. Hold back ¾ cup of mixture. Lightly oil a leather sheet and spread all but the ¾ cup banana mixture onto the sheet and flatten. Spread the remaining ¾ cup on the top. Dehydrate at 105 degrees until it is able to hold its shape. Generally after 2 hours, transfer it to the mesh sheet and dry until firm.

To make the filling, soak the macadamia nuts in enough water to cover for 30 minutes. Put all remaining ingredients in a blender and grind. Add soaked, drained nuts and blend until smooth.

To put the omelet together, spread the filling on one side of the shell, top with carrots, cilantro, onions, and avocado. Fold and enjoy!

POWDERING DRIED FOODS
JONI'S ASPARAGUS SOUP • BEST BORSCHT

CELERY AND TOMATOES

CORN
CORN MUFFINS

EGGPLANT
DIPPING SOLUTION • MULANZAN • DOLMAS
MOUSSAKA • BABA GHANOUJ

GREENS
KALE FLAKES

MUSHROOMS
YUMMY BUTTER • MUSHROOM PÂTÉ

ONIONS
PRETTY AND DELICIOUS ONION MIX

PEPPERS
PEPPER PURÉE • HOT PEPPER JELLY

PUMPKIN AND WINTER SQUASH
MY VERSION OF BUFFALO BIRD WOMAN'S DISH • SQUASH BLOSSOMS

SUNFLOWERS

TOMATOES
OLIVE OIL AND DRIED TOMATOES • HALF-DRIED TOMATO SPREAD
TOMATO GARBANZO SALAD • STUFFED VEGETABLE LOAF
• VEGETABLE BEEF STEW

ZUCCHINI
ZUCCHINI-RHUBARB BREAD • ZUCCHINI CHIPS

Vegetables

Drying Vegetables

After all these years of drying food, for me the drying of vegetables is still the most exciting and diverse area of creative culinary expression. While compiling this book, I fell in love with dried eggplant. So much of what I learned over the years came to fruition with the eggplant we grew in our garden. The sixteen plants produced at least four eggplants each and I dried all that we didn't eat fresh. Next year I'm planting thirty-two plants and will sell dried eggplant at our farmers' market.

After the tilling of the soil, the planting, and the pulling of weeds comes the reward of the harvest. Having once planted a whole package of zucchini seeds, I know that harvest time can be overwhelming, and I am so grateful that I found the option of drying. Drying is a wonderful way to preserve seasonal crops, save money, and enjoy great food all year long.

The challenge in drying, especially with vegetables, is in thinking about the end product. It is helpful to determine how you intend to use the food before you begin drying it because this can change how you prepare it for drying. Ask yourself, will it be eaten dry, powdered, or rehydrated? For example, if you intend to serve corn as a side dish, it will rehydrate faster and taste better if it is blanched before being dried. If you plan on using corn for cornmeal, don't blanch it because you are just going to grind it up anyway.

Drying Vegetables is Easy

This A to Z chapter begins with asparagus and ends with zucchini. The following instructions should provide a good basis for drying just about any vegetable.

Vegetables are washed and sliced in $\frac{1}{8}$- to $\frac{1}{4}$-inch pieces. There are some vegetables that rehydrate faster and taste better if they are blanched. Blanching can be done by steam, in boiling water, or using a microwave. I blanch asparagus spears, broccoli, brussels sprouts, carrots, cauliflower, green beans, and peas. I also blanch beets to remove the skins, corn when I want to use it as a side dish, potatoes to minimize darkening, and rhubarb to eliminate some acidity.

> To preserve color I dip potatoes, cauliflower, brussels sprouts, cabbage, broccoli, and kohlrabi in lemon juice. I dip eggplant in a combination of salt and lemon juice. Salt helps to pull water from food, keeps it lighter in color, and is a preservative that promotes longer shelf life.

Raw Talk

Raw foods are rich sources of enzymes. People involved in the raw food movement want to protect the heat-sensitive enzymes in food. Although there is debate regarding the temperature at which food should be dried, most agree that a temperature of 110 degrees or below is best, although some say 120 degrees.

In a raw food kitchen, you can't bake food in an oven, cook on a stovetop, or put food in a microwave oven. So dehydrators are used for making bread, cookies, muffins, brownies, bars, chips, and crackers, as well as to warm food. Dehydrators provide a means to control and manipulate the liquid in food, to enhance flavor, and to alter the texture of food.

For those less concerned about enzymes in fruits and vegetables, the recommended drying temperature for vegetables and fruit is between 130 and 140 degrees. At 135 degrees, $\frac{1}{4}$- to $\frac{1}{2}$-inch food pieces dry in 8 to 12 hours. It will take longer to dry food at lower temperatures. Remember to dry vegetables until hard; otherwise, they can mold if they are not kept in the freezer. Fruits, especially ripe ones, contain sugar and do not need to be dried as hard because sugar acts as a natural preservative.

> Raw food chefs use dehydrators to make exciting foods that are on the cutting edge of culinary creativity. Chicago chef Charlie Trotter's wildly inventive dried blue cheese is intensely flavorful in salads.

Half-drying

Years ago, while researching the history of food, I learned that the Romans dried meat in their ovens for just a little while in order to dry off the surface water. Then they would marinate the meat in various liquids and spices to embolden the flavor.

A dehydrator lets you eliminate some or all of the water in food. You have the option of stopping the drying process at any time. By removing just the surface water of a fruit or vegetable you can intensify and concentrate the taste and make the texture firmer. This is what I call half-drying, which is another exciting way to use a dehydrator and create exotic new and different foods.

Another benefit of half-drying is that you can marinate the half-dried food in various liquids and the food will absorb more marinade or flavoring. This is more effective than marinating food that already has enough water. By controlling the water in food, you have enormous control over the food itself. Imagine a purple mushroom that has been soaked in burgundy wine or a tomato that tastes like a dill pickle. Consider slicing a mango, half-drying it, then marinating it in amaretto. Make an orange apple by removing the surface moisture, then soaking it in orange juice before drying it.

> **Be aware:** *If half or partially dry food is not eaten right away, it must be kept in the refrigerator or stored in the freezer for the long-term.*

Rehydrating

Drying removes water from food. The process of putting it back is called rehydration. Once rehydrated, many dried foods are indistinguishable from the fresh original. Cooked dried spinach will taste garden fresh. However, not all dried food will be exactly like it was when it was fresh, nor will everybody like the taste, flavor, or texture of everything you rehydrate. You need to experiment to find out which vegetables you enjoy rehydrated.

Rehydration time depends on the size and type of food: generally 15 minutes for ¼-inch pieces and 1 hour for larger pieces. The larger the piece, the longer it takes to rehydrate. Warm liquids reduce rehydration time.

Pre-treated, blanched food rehydrates faster. Some vegetables, like carrots, can toughen when placed directly in boiling liquid, whereas eggplant rehydrates beautifully when placed in boiling water. Simmer dried fruit to soften and plump up. Rehydrated foods should be eaten right away.

Dried foods do not need to be rehydrated before they are added to soups, stews, and casseroles that have adequate liquid.

In addition to using water as a rehydration liquid, you can use juices, broths, and liquors to create rich and unique flavors. Rehydrate dried corn in milk. Soak dried apples in cranberry juice. Marinate dried mushrooms in wine and chicken broth.

Powdering Dried Foods

Turning dried food into powder creates bold, concentrated, rich, all-natural foods. Drying takes water out of food, greatly reducing its volume and intensifying its taste. By grinding dried food into a powder, it is reduced even further, leaving only the absolute essence of the food.

Making powders is a great way to save food and money. Instead of throwing away the tough ends of asparagus, dry them. Same thing goes for woody mushroom stems. Once the fibrous stems and tough ends have been dried and pulverized into a powder in a blender, you will not be able

to tell the tough end from the asparagus tip or the mushroom stem from the mushroom cap.

To make a powder, you need a blender, coffee grinder, or food processor, and food that has been dried hard. Over the years, I have used many brands and various sizes of blenders, and they all work. A blender that has a small container (like a mason jar) works especially well. Simply blend the dried food until pulverized and store in airtight containers.

Powders are a great way to use food as flavoring instead of using salt, sugar, or other seasonings. Powders make dynamite additions to soups, sauces, omelets, and baby food. Add powdered dried spinach, asparagus, or chestnut flour to cream soup. Add powders to pudding, ice cream, cakes, breads, and smoothies. In the cold of winter, strawberry powder adds pizzazz to boring breakfast oatmeal. Banana flour can become a milk substitute. Put a tablespoon of peach powder in your angel food cake batter. Sprinkle fruit powders on popcorn. Spoon dried strawberry powder on ice cream and add to yogurt. After you've squeezed lemons for lemonade, dry the peels and make 100 percent lemon powder to use in baking, especially for frosting. Use tomato, spinach, and mushroom powder as a flour when making homemade noodles.

Powdering dried food greatly reduces the amount of storage space required. For example, a jar of 20 dried tomatoes becomes 1 ½ cups tomato powder. Tomato powder can become a sauce, a soup, or a paste depending on how much water you use. Or you can simply sprinkle the tomato powder over a salad.

Dried foods that contain sugar or that are not dried hard enough may require an extra step before turning them into powders. Tomatoes and strawberries often fit in this category. To make powder out of these foods, put them in a plastic bag and place in the freezer for one hour because cold, crisp dried food is easier to grind.

Dried powdered beets add color and sweetness to hummingbird feeders. I also dry and powder corn intended for cornmeal, the peels of eggplant and zucchini, and the stems and ribs from any greens. Radish powder spices up a salad dressing.

In addition to eating dried food dry, you can rehydrate it in various liquids, or you can put it in a blender and powder it.

JONI'S ASPARAGUS SOUP

When I asked my Thursday morning yoga group who had the best asparagus soup recipe, all fingers pointed to Joni Finnegan. Her recipe is terrific with other dried foods added, especially dried morel and shiitake mushrooms. This is a "no-waste" situation. Cut unwanted asparagus stems in ¼-inch pieces and dry until hard. Grind the stems until fine. If necessary use a strainer to separate out any big pieces. Half a cup of powder equals 24 fresh asparagus spears. Dried, blanched asparagus spears can be added after the broth has been blended. | Makes 6 servings.

- 1 pound fresh chicken breasts, cut in ½-inch pieces • 3 tablespoons olive oil
- 1 cup celery, sliced thin • 1 cup onions, chopped fine • 5 cups chicken stock
- ½ cup dried asparagus powder • 1 teaspoon lemon thyme, finely chopped
- ⅛ teaspoon black pepper • 1 cup whipping cream • ½ cup sour cream
- 1 teaspoon lemon rind • Juice of 1 lemon

In a large sauté pan, fry chicken in 2 tablespoons oil. Remove from pan and place in a bowl. In the sauté pan, add remaining oil and sauté celery and onions until soft. Add chicken stock and asparagus powder. Stir and bring to a boil, reduce heat, and simmer 5 minutes. Remove from heat. Cool and blend in a blender. Return soup to pan, add cooked chicken, thyme, and pepper, and simmer 10 minutes.

Whip the cream. Fold in sour cream, lemon rind, and juice. Spoon dollops on top of warm soup.

BEST BORSCHT

Christian Milaster and Jennifer Meadows built an awesome environmentally conscious home in southeastern Minnesota. The house design reflects a commitment to living a sustainable lifestyle that includes eating locally

grown food. We adapted Jennifer's favorite borscht recipe to use with dried beets. Boil beets to remove the skins. For this recipe I peeled and shredded the beets, then dried them crisp and crushed them by hand. | Makes 4 to 6 servings.

• 1 cup dried beets, shredded and crushed • 4 cups chicken stock • 2 tablespoons lemon juice • 3 tablespoons honey • 2 teaspoons dried dill weed • 1 medium cucumber, peeled, seeded, and grated • 3 scallions, finely minced • 1 medium-sized dill pickle, finely minced • ⅛ teaspoon black pepper • 2 cups buttermilk

Place dried beets in a soup pan with chicken stock and let rehydrate 30 minutes. Bring to a boil and add lemon juice, honey, and dill weed. Refrigerate until cool. Place one half of the beets in a blender. Return to pan, add cucumber, scallions, pickle, and pepper. Stir. Fold in buttermilk. Cover and re-chill until cold. Top with any combination of garnishes.

> Garnishes for the Borscht • *Fat free yogurt* • *Sour cream* • *Chopped hardboiled eggs* • *Boiled potato cubes*

CELERY AND TOMATOES

Real celery powder and fresh, garden tomato slices are meant for each other.

• 2 cups fresh tomatoes, chopped • 1 tablespoon fresh basil, chopped • 1 tablespoon balsamic vinegar • ½ teaspoon sugar • 1 teaspoon dried celery powder

Combine tomatoes, basil, vinegar, and sugar in a bowl. Let sit 15 minutes. Sprinkle celery powder on top and serve.

> Celery is one of those foods we buy over and over again. I've talked to many people who admit discarding unused celery, then going back to the store for more. There is another option! Fresh, perfect, and even limp celery can be dried and saved. Cut celery into ¼-inch pieces and place on a mesh-lined drying tray. Dry until hard and grind to a powder in a blender. Homemade celery powder is a fantastic, aromatic, salt-free, 100 percent natural seasoning.

Corn

Corn has been one of the most important crops ever grown. For my mentor, Buffalo Bird Woman, any corn that wasn't eaten fresh was dried. Some was ground into meal. Some corn was dried and braided and either hung in their homes or cached in grass-lined earthen pits. In addition to using the kernels, they burned the cobs, and the ash was a favorite seasoning. The silk was dried and used as a thickening agent. Even the corn smut fungus was dried and used to flavor soups and stews.

> When corn is destined for use as a side dish, blanch it on the cob and cut off the kernels. If you intend to use the dried corn for cornmeal, simply cut the kernels off the cob without blanching, dry until hard, and grind in the blender.

CORN MUFFINS

Heidi Dybing's environmental sensitivity was the reason she left the big city and moved to a farm. She is a fantastic cook and baker and raises 95 percent of her family's food, including organic beef, chicken, pork, and eggs. This is her recipe for perfect corn muffins.

- 1 ½ teaspoons cornmeal • ¾ cup unbleached flour • ½ teaspoon baking powder
- ¼ teaspoon salt • ⅛ teaspoon baking soda • ¼ cup cheddar cheese, shredded
- 1 tablespoon butter, melted • ½ cup sour milk • 2 tablespoons green onion
- 1 small clove garlic, chopped • 1 egg, slightly beaten • extra cheddar

Mix cornmeal, flour, baking powder, salt, and soda together in a bowl. Stir in cheese, butter, and milk. Put onion and garlic in a small bowl. Add egg and whisk. Combine the two mixtures and stir just until moist. Pour in well-greased muffin tins. Sprinkle a little cheddar on top. Bake at 375 degrees. Bake 6 regular muffins for 18 to 20 minutes. For 20 mini muffins, bake 12 minutes. Remove from tins immediately.

Eggplant

Eggplant is an excellent example of how to prepare one food in a variety of ways for drying. The criteria for determining how to dry are based on how you plan to use it: peel or don't peel, cut in slices or rounds, dip or don't dip. When you peel the eggplant you can dry the peelings until they are hard, grind to a powder in the blender, and use as a flavoring.

As I experimented with eggplant, I found that I preferred using dried eggplant rather than fresh. Dried eggplant doesn't need as much oil for frying. Just cook it and then dip one side in oil and proceed with any recipe. Dried eggplant can also be used as a substitute in pasta—try eggplant lasagna.

DIPPING SOLUTION

This solution also works well with zucchini.

• 2 cups water • 1 heaping tablespoon salt • 1 tablespoon lemon juice

Put eggplant, one piece at a time, in the dipping solution and make sure all surfaces have been coated. Put a plate on top of the eggplant to weigh the pieces down and let sit at least 1 hour. Remove and place the strips on a mesh-lined dehydrator tray and dry at 135 degrees until hard. Dried eggplant absorbs moisture from the air very quickly, so it is important to store the dried eggplant in airtight containers as soon as it has cooled.

For mulanzan: peel, slice in rounds, dip, and dry.

For dolmas: peel, slice in long (3-by-8-inch) strips, dip, and dry.

For moussaka: cut in long strips, leave peelings on, dip, and dry.

For baba ghanouj: peel, don't dip, then dry.

When I was drying the eggplant several slices fell to the floor and before I could pick them up our dogs walked away with them and proceeded to devour them. I do not know if dogs should or shouldn't eat eggplant, but ours liked it a lot.

MULANZAN

Dried eggplant in the shape of rounds work best when making mulanzan. Serve this southern Italian dried eggplant appetizer and meat substitute on crackers.

• 4 cups olive oil • 2 teaspoons dried oregano • 2 teaspoons dried basil • 1 teaspoon dried parsley • 8 cloves, fresh garlic • 1 cup red wine vinegar • 1 ounce fresh hot red peppers, cut in circles • 48 3-inch dried eggplant rounds

Mix oil, dried herbs, garlic, vinegar, and peppers in a bowl. Pour ½ cup of the oil mixture into a large-mouth storage jar with a tight-fitting lid. Place one dried eggplant slice into the jar at a time. With a large spoon press the slices gently into the oil so each one is covered. Continue adding eggplant and cover with oil. Top the container with extra oil to keep the slices submerged. Let the jar lid remain a tiny bit ajar to allow any gas to escape. You might notice a green color after a few days. That's normal. This mixture should marinate three weeks and turn brown in color. Keep tightly covered and store in the refrigerator.

DOLMAS

This is an eggplant version of stuffed grape leaves.

- 2 cups water • 12 3-by-8-inch slices dried eggplant
- 2 tablespoons olive oil • ¼ cup onion, chopped
- 2 tablespoons peppers, chopped • ½ pound ground meat (lamb or beef) • 2 cloves garlic, mashed • 2 tablespoons raisins
- ½ teaspoon cinnamon • ½ teaspoon allspice • 2 tablespoons parsley, chopped • 1 tablespoon lemon juice • ½ cup rice, cooked • 2 cups canned tomatoes • ⅛ teaspoon dried basil
- ⅛ teaspoon dried oregano

Place eggplant slices one at a time in boiling water for 3 to 5 minutes, until the slices become soft without falling apart. Remove with a slotted spoon or use tongs. Lay the eggplant flat on a cutting board and let it cool.

Place oil in sauté pan and add onion and garlic. Stir. Add meat and cook until it is in small pieces. Add all remaining ingredients, except rice, tomatoes, basil, and oregano. Remove from heat, cool, and add rice.

Put canned tomatoes in saucepan and crush the tomatoes with your hands. Add basil and oregano and stir.

Open a slice of softened eggplant and spoon the meat mixture on top. Roll and seal with two toothpicks. Put the stuffed eggplant in with the tomato sauce, cover, and simmer on low heat for 15 to 30 minutes.

MOUSSAKA

This is simply an eggplant casserole. I like to use dried eggplant slices that have some peeling left on to add color and texture. | Makes 4 to 6 servings.

- 2 tablespoons dried bell pepper pieces, ¼-inch thick • 3 tablespoons water
- 2 tablespoons olive oil • 1 cup onion, chopped fine • 1 tablespoon garlic • 1 pound ground meat (lamb or beef) • 2 tablespoons dried parsley, crushed • ½ teaspoon ground cinnamon • ¼ teaspoon ground cloves • ¼ teaspoon nutmeg • 3 cups canned tomatoes • 3 cups water • 24 2-by-7-inch dried eggplant slices • 2 cups ricotta cheese
- 3 egg whites, beaten • ½ cup Parmesan cheese

Put pepper pieces and water in a bowl and rehydrate 30 minutes. Put oil and onion in a pan and sauté for 3 minutes. Stir. Add rehydrated peppers and garlic. Stir. Add ground meat and work to break it into small pieces. Add parsley, cinnamon, cloves, nutmeg, and sauté until well browned. Add tomatoes and simmer until most of the liquid evaporates. Remove from heat.

Bring 3 cups water to a boil. Add dried eggplant slices one at a time and with a slotted spoon or tongs remove the slices as soon as they have softened. Generally this takes around 5 minutes. Remove slices and lay them flat on a cutting board and let cool.

Beat egg whites and gently fold into the cheese.

Oil the inside of a casserole dish. Dip the eggplant slices in a little olive oil, then layer the slices in the dish with an extra layer on the bottom, then a layer of meat mixture, a layer of cheese, another layer of eggplant, repeating until all ingredients are used. Top with Parmesan cheese. Bake at 325 degrees for 40 minutes covered, then remove cover and bake 20 minutes more or until the top turns golden. Allow time to cool before serving.

BABA GHANOUJ

This traditional eggplant dip is great with pita bread. | Makes ½ cup.

- 1 cup dried eggplant, 1-inch pieces
- ½ cup boiling water • 3 tablespoons tahini • 1 tablespoon lemon juice
- 1 tablespoon olive oil • 1 teaspoon garlic, chopped • ½ teaspoon cumin
- 2 tablespoons fresh parsley, chopped fine

Pour boiling water over the eggplant pieces, push down to submerge, and let stand at least 1 hour. Drain off and discard rehyhdration liquid. Put eggplant in blender and purée. Add tahini, lemon juice, oil, garlic, and cumin. Blend again. Refrigerate at least 3 hours. Top with parsley before serving.

Greens

Greens dry beautifully. Add dried kale, spinach, and Swiss chard to eggs, soup, sauces, and casseroles. Thick internal stems or large internal ribs must be cut out and can be dried separately.

My friend Tricia Yu dries gallons of kale each year. She crushes the dried leaves into flakes and adds them to soups and stews (split pea, lentil, chicken, and turkey), to quiches, dips, sprinkles flakes on pizza, and puts dried kale in anything that calls for spinach, including her morning omelet and oatmeal. She said, "I generally eat greens for breakfast. You simply never know what foods the rest of your day will bring." Tricia is a master tai chi practitioner and has always lived a healthy and balanced lifestyle.

KALE FLAKES

Turn kale into light, crunchy, and healthy chip-like flakes. The curly variety, once dry, just about melts in your mouth.

- 3 tablespoons apple cider vinegar • 1 teaspoon salt
- 1 tablespoon olive oil • 2 cups kale, cut in 1- to 2-inch strips or cubes

Choose young kale. Clean. Cut away the internal stems. They too can be dried and powdered, but they make the chips too tough if they are not removed. My first cut is the tip of the leaf of young kale that doesn't have much of an internal stem. Then I cut along the internal stem into 2-inch pieces or long strips. When finished, you will have lettuce-like kale pieces and a stripped internal stem that you can dry separately and grind into a powder. Tender young chard or spinach leaves work just as well as kale.

Place vinegar, salt, and oil in a bowl. Stir. Add kale and mix by hand to get the surface of all leaves covered. Place a bowl on top of the marinating kale to force it into the marinade and let sit for 1 hour. Flatten each leaf on mesh-lined dehydrator sheets. Sprinkle lightly with salt and dry at 110 to 135 degrees until crisp.

> **Tricia Yu's Sauce for Life** "I raised my child on this recipe. I use it as a dip, a sandwich spread, for salad dressing, and as a sauce when I bake fish. It goes on everything!" Tricia says.

- 3 cups non-fat yogurt • 1 cup mayonnaise • 2 tablespoons dehydrated crushed kale
- 2 tablespoons dehydrated onion flakes • 1 tablespoon dehydrated garlic granules
- 1 tablespoon dried dill weed

Mix together and let sit in refrigerator for at least 1 hour so it has time to thicken.

> **Variation** *Prepare leaves, place in a bowl, pour vinegar over leaves, press down to force vinegar into leaves, and marinate at least 1 hour. Remove from marinade and toss with olive oil. Place on a mesh-lined dehydrator or oiled leather sheet. Instead of separating each sheet, allow the leaves to overlap. Sprinkle with salt and dry.*

Mushrooms

Mushrooms dry incredibly well and last for years in airtight containers. Positive identification of all wild mushrooms is a must. If you are not absolutely sure the mushroom is edible, do not even consider it.

Mushrooms stay lighter in color if they are not washed before being dried. However, some mushrooms, like wild morels, need to be cleaned of dirt and bugs.

When rehydrating mushrooms, strain the rehydration liquid through cheesecloth to capture all the mushroom bits and to separate out any unwanted debris.

Hunting Morels on Horseback *We were on a trail ride one spring day when my husband said, "Mary, what do you see?" I looked around, didn't notice anything out of the ordinary, looked at him, and shrugged my shoulders. He said, "Look down." Everywhere there were scads of morel mushrooms, some bigger than my hand. It was a dream come true. I had always wanted to go mushroom hunting on horseback. We smiled at each other and high-tailed it home for recycled plastic shopping bags and quickly headed back to our found treasure. We picked and picked, wrapped the bags around our saddle horns, and gleefully trotted home. We ended up with five pounds of dried morels that fed us for several years and made great gifts.*

YUMMY BUTTER

You can serve this versatile butter on top of cooked vegetables, use it to sauté vegetables, add it to pasta, and serve it on crackers.

• ¼ cup mushroom powder • 2 teaspoons warm water • ½ cup butter

Place mushroom powder in a small bowl with warm water and rehydrate 2 minutes. Melt butter on medium heat, add mushrooms, and sauté 3 minutes. Season to taste. Pour into container and refrigerate. Remove 30 minutes before using to allow time to soften.

MUSHROOM PÂTÉ

This recipe works best when the mushrooms are coarsely ground. Substitute any dried mushroom as well as any nut—almonds, walnuts, pecans, sunflower seeds, and toasted nuts all work well.

• ½ cup shiitake mushroom pieces, coarsely ground • ½ cup white wine • 3 tablespoons butter • ¾ cup nuts • 1 8-ounce package cream cheese • 1 teaspoon dried parsley, crushed

Place mushrooms and wine in a blender. Let sit 10 minutes. Grind to small, rice-like pieces. Melt butter in a medium-sized sauté pan and add rehydrated mushroom pieces. Sauté until liquid evaporates. Add nuts and blend. Remove from heat and add cream cheese. Because the pan is hot,

the cream cheese will combine easily. Blend thoroughly.

Line a bowl with plastic wrap. Pat the mushroom mixture into the bowl. Chill in the refrigerator at least 1 hour before serving.

Crush parsley and sprinkle on top. Serve with crackers.

Onions

Onions, especially strong-smelling ones, may require wearing goggles and finding a drying area outside of the house. Set your dehydrator on the porch or in the garage if the smells get too strong. Note that you do not want to put the dehydrator in a place where the wind can impact the drying process. To dry an onion, peel the outer skin away, chop into ¼-inch pieces, and dry on mesh-lined dehydrator trays.

PRETTY AND DELICIOUS ONION MIX

Dry onions until hard; cool and mix together in an airtight container. This combination makes a practically instant and very flavorful blend. Put in a jar, tie a bow around it, attach a recipe, and give as a gift. Grind onions to a powder and add to sour cream for a chip dip.

Peppers

You may want to put the dehydrator someplace other than your kitchen when drying hot peppers. Cut any variety of peppers into the size pieces you ultimately want to use. I like ¼-inch pieces to use in soups, casseroles, salads, and stews. To dry peppers whole, poke holes all the way through the skin so dry air can get inside.

Dried Roasted Peppers *Keep the fresh, sweet, red pepper whole, leaving the stem intact. Rinse. Preheat a gas grill. Hold the peppers with tongs, shuffling and turning peppers over the flames until they are mostly charred and blackened. Put in a paper bag or airtight container to "sweat," which loosens the blackened skins as the peppers cool. This makes it easier to shed their skins. Split the peppers and keep the seeds and core intact (the heart is the source of flavor, nutri-*  *ents, and texture). Remove stem. Place pepper halves on a mesh-lined drying tray. Dry until leathery or half dry. If half dry, use right away or store in the freezer. Sliver the dried peppers with kitchen scissors, or cut in cubes or slices. Use dried roasted peppers like sun-dried tomatoes in salads, wraps, pasta dishes, soups, stews, and stir fries.*

PEPPER PURÉE

Kitty Baker, our nearest neighbor—a mile away as the crow flies—makes it a priority to use locally grown food. Everything she cooks looks like it should be on the cover of a gourmet food magazine. This is one of her favorite, yet simple and romantic, creations.

- 2 blackened, skinned, dried peppers
- ½ tablespoon red wine vinegar • 2 toasted garlic cloves, mashed

Place all ingredients in a blender and process until smooth.

This pepper purée is great in salad dressing and in stir fry, rice, and pasta dishes. Try spreading it over room-temperature Brie or Camembert cheese and serve with seed-coated crackers. Place a dollop of purée in a shallow dish, top with good olive oil and fresh-ground pepper, and use as a dip for gourmet bread slices.

Jams and Jellies

Making jam and jelly from dried foods is a wonderful way to keep sweets in your pantry. However, slaving over a hot stove during the dog days of summer often deters people from taking on this task. Instead, dry fresh food when it is in season and then make jams and jellies on cold winter days when a little extra heat in the house is welcome.

HOT PEPPER JELLY

Top a cracker with cream cheese and add a spot of pepper jelly. Serve hot pepper jelly as an accompaniment to beef, pork, or lamb. Try a combination of red hot peppers, sweet yellow banana peppers, and green peppers. Seeds and stems must be removed from dried peppers. When preparing hot peppers, be careful not to touch your eyes or lips. | Makes 6 half-pints.

- 1/3 cup dried hot peppers, coarsely ground • ¼ cup dried bell pepper, coarsely ground
- 2 cups water • 2 cups apple cider vinegar • 1.17-ounce package Sure-Jell
- 1 cup fresh onion, finely chopped • ½ teaspoon salt • 4 cups sugar

In a 4-quart pan, combine peppers and water. Stir. Let sit 1 hour. Bring to a boil. Remove from heat and add vinegar. Stir. Cover and let sit 1 more hour. Place in a blender to break up into small pieces. To complete this recipe, you need 4 cups of liquid, so you may have to add a little more water to get that quantity.

Return the pepper juice to the pan, add the onion and salt, and simmer until the onions become translucent, about 5 to 10 minutes. Then, bring to a boil over high heat, stirring constantly.

When a rolling boil is reached, add sugar and boil hard for 1 minute. Add Sure-Jell, stir, and when it reaches full boil again, cook exactly one minute. Remove from heat. Skim off any foam. Ladle hot jelly into hot, sterilized jars, filling to ¼-inch from the top.

Wipe jar rims and threads. Cover. Screw bands tightly. Place in canner and make sure jars are covered by 1 to 2 inches of water. Cover the canner and bring water to a gentle boil. Then process 5 minutes. Remove jars carefully and place upright on a towel to cool completely. Once cool, check seals by pressing middle of lid with finger, they should not spring back

---

Yummy Snack *1 8-ounce package cream cheese, softened* • *½ cup hot pepper jelly*
- *Mix together or put cream cheese on cracker and top with jelly.*

Pumpkin and Winter Squash

Peel the pumpkins or winter squash, remove the seeds, cut in ½-inch cubes, sprinkle with lemon juice, and dry at 135 degrees. This is how I dried butternut squash for a five-day horseback pack trip we took into the Grand Canyon. When we reached the upper canyon, we made camp under a rock overhang that looked like an Anasazi cave. Dinner that night was rehydrated dried squash. Eating this meal in this very spiritual place gave us an incredible sense of history.

Buffalo Bird Woman dried squash in the traditional manner. She picked squash just before sunrise so the slices would stay firm and retain their shape during the drying process. Bone squash knives, which were made from green (freshly butchered) bones, were used only for slicing squash because they kept an edge. Squash slices were cut ½-inch thick. The seed cavity became the hollow center that was threaded onto willow rod poles that were hung on the drying stage. Slices were kept about a half-inch apart to give each slice air to dry.

Buffalo Bird Woman dried food when the wind was strong and the sun was hot. Once dry, the squash slices were threaded on grass strings, taken into the lodge, and hung in the driest air. This harvesting and drying process took about one month to complete.

Buffalo Bird Woman's Four-vegetables-mixed *Four-vegetables-mixed was Buffalo Bird Woman's favorite dish. Into a clay pot with water, she threw "one double-handful of beans and put on fire." Once the beans were soft she cut a piece of strung dried squash, "as long as from my elbow to the tip of my thumb." When the squash slices were cooked, she removed the squash with a horn spoon, mashed the squash, and returned it to the pot with beans. Then she added four to five double-handfuls of mixed meal, pounded sunflower seed, and pounded parched corn. It was brought to a boil and when ready for serving, she added two or three double-handfuls of parched sunflower seed.*

MY VERSION OF BUFFALO BIRD WOMAN'S DISH

Makes 4 servings.

• ½ cup white navy beans • 3 cups chicken broth • ½ cup dried squash cubes • ½ cup sunflower seeds, coarsely ground • ¼ cup cornmeal • ¼ teaspoon black pepper

Soak beans overnight in 1 cup broth. Cook until beans soften. Add the remaining ingredients and cook until squash softens and most of the liquid evaporates. Mash and serve with butter.

Squash Blossoms

Dried squash blossoms were considered a gourmet item that Buffalo Bird Woman used to flavor various dishes. Blossoms were picked early in the morning, put in baskets, and laid on "antelope hair" grass. "The blossoms were taken out of the basket one by one; the green calyx leaves were stripped off and the blossom was pinched flat, then opened and spread on the grass, with the inside of the blossom upward, thus exposing it to the sun and air. A second blossom was split on one side, opened, and laid upon the first, upon the petal end, so that the thicker, bulbous part of the first—the part indeed that had been pinched flat—remained exposed to dry. Splitting them open

---

Dried corn, dried squash, and dried beans were the dietary staples for Buffalo Bird Woman and her people. To dry beans, Buffalo Bird Woman made a carpet of corn stalks on which she laid ripened bean pods. After they dried for several days, she transferred the beans to a tent cover that served as her threshing floor. "I took up some of the dry vines and laid them in a heap, about three feet high. I got upon this heap with my moccasined feet and smartly trampled it, now and then standing on one foot, while I shuffled and scraped the other over the dry vines to shake the beans loose from their pods. When the vines were pretty well trampled I pushed them over two or three feet to one side of the tent cover; and having fetched fresh vines, I made another heap about three feet high, which I also trampled and pushed aside. When I had trampled three or four heaps in this manner I was ready to beat them. I always threshed my beans on a windy day if possible, so that I might winnow them immediately after threshing. After the beans were winnowed, they were dried one more day and then packed in sacks."

and laying them down one upon another caused them to adhere as they dried so that they lay on the grass in a kind of thin matting and would come off in one sheet."

Sunflowers

Sunflowers were the first crop Buffalo Bird Woman planted in the spring and the last she harvested in the fall. The heads were cut when the little petals that covered the seeds fell off and exposed the ripe seeds. The cut heads were laid on the ground facing down so the backs were to the sun. The sun's heat dried and shrunk the fibers and loosened the seeds. Once dry, the heads were beaten with a stick, the seeds were collected and roasted or parched, then ground using a mortar and pestle.

Tomatoes

People always ask what I do with dried tomatoes. I used to say, "Use dried tomatoes in everything but a bacon, lettuce, and tomato sandwich." Well, one time a guy replied, "I'd rather have a dried tomato in my BLT than a tomato that doesn't have any flavor." I stand corrected. Dried tomatoes are also great in spaghetti sauces, soups, stews, and casseroles, and with eggs.

All varieties, even green tomatoes, can be dried. Meaty tomatoes like Roma and Celebrity are great for drying. Choose firm tomatoes that have just turned red. Do not dry too-ripe tomatoes because they darken. Wash. Remove stem. Peeling is optional (I don't). If you choose to peel, immerse tomatoes in boiling water for about 15 seconds, then quickly plunge into cold water and the skins should slip off easily. Cut tomatoes into ¼-inch slices or rounds. The thicker the piece, the longer it will take to dry. Place on a mesh-lined dehydrator tray and dry until crisp at a temperature no higher than 135 degrees.

Olive Oil and Dried Tomatoes

When packing dried tomatoes with oil, use sterilized wide mouth quart jars and press down with a wooden spoon to squeeze out any air pockets. Layer tomatoes, add oil, and then more tomatoes. Leave at least one inch of headspace at the top of each jar so the tomatoes remain submerged in oil. Store in the refrigerator. The oil may congeal but will soften if the bottle is left out on the counter for a few minutes before using. Serve on lettuce or spinach, add to cooked pasta, and use in cooking. This olive oil has absorbed the tomato flavor and also tastes great.

HALF-DRIED TOMATO SPREAD

• 4 cups half-dried tomatoes (see directions below) • 4 tablespoons olive oil • 1 tablespoon honey • 2 cloves garlic, minced • 1 tablespoon balsamic vinegar • ½ teaspoon dried basil or fresh, cut in strips • ½ teaspoon dried oregano • ¼ teaspoon salt

Cut fresh tomatoes in 1-inch chunks. Dry until the surface moisture has evaporated. The skins will be wrinkly and the tomato chunks will have

reduced to about half the original size. Generally this takes about 5 hours when dried at 135 degrees. In addition to serving this as an appetizer, enjoy over cooked pasta, on crackers, on open lettuce leaves, or as an accompaniment to meat.

Mix ingredients together and refrigerate.

TOMATO GARBANZO SALAD

This salad is made with a combination of half-dried and fully dried tomatoes. You can do the same with half and fully dried peppers and mushrooms. Artichokes are a nice addition to this salad. | Makes 4 servings.

- ½ cup sweet white wine • ½ cup dried tomatoes, crushed • ½ cup dried mushroom slices
- 2 tablespoons dried bell peppers, ¼-inch cubes • 2 tablespoons balsamic vinegar
- 2 tablespoons sesame oil • 1 tablespoon honey • 1 tablespoon garlic, mashed
- 1 ½ cups garbanzo beans, cooked and strained • ½ cup celery, chopped fine
- ½ cup olives, chopped fine • ¼ cup half dried tomatoes • ¼ cup onion, chopped fine
- ½ teaspoon dried basil • ¼ teaspoon rosemary, crushed • ¼ teaspoon salt
- ¼ teaspoon pepper, coarsely ground • Lettuce leaves • ¼ cup Parmesan cheese

Place wine, tomatoes, mushrooms, peppers, vinegar, oil, honey, and garlic in a bowl. Stir. Let it rehydrate for at least 1 hour. Longer marinating time allows dried vegetables more time to soften. Add garbanzo beans, celery, olives, half dried tomatoes, onion, basil, rosemary, salt, and pepper. Stir. Serve on lettuce leaves. Top with cheese.

STUFFED VEGETABLE LOAF

I have been making versions of this loaf for thirty years and most recently when I gave this recipe to my friend, Nancy Martinson, she made it even better. This easy and elegant dish is a great potluck offering. Substitute black olives for green ones, and tomato powder for fresh tomatoes. | Makes 4 to 8 servings.

- ½ cup dried tomatoes, crushed • ⅓ cup Spanish olive juice • ⅔ cup water • 3 tablespoons olive oil • ½ cup Spanish olives, sliced • ¼ cup half-dried olive slices • ½ cup onion, diced • 1 cup tomatoes, diced • ¼ teaspoon salt • ¼ teaspoon pepper • ⅛ teaspoon dried rosemary • ⅛ teaspoon dried thyme • 1 loaf French bread or 2 baguettes

Soak dry tomatoes in olive juice and water for 2 hours. Add olive oil, olives, onion, tomatoes, salt, pepper, rosemary, and thyme. Stir. Cut bread in half horizontally. Hollow out the inside of each half leaving a shell approximately ¾-inch thick. Break the removed bread into ½-inch pieces and add to the vegetable mixture. Stir well. Stuff the bread with the mixture and press the stuffed halves together and wrap in aluminum foil. Refrigerate 4 hours before serving. Slice and serve.

VEGETABLE BEEF STEW

Slow cookers are wonderful rehydration appliances, especially when time in the kitchen is limited. This stew is a meal everyone loves. When you walk into the house on a cold winter day, the smell alone feeds your soul before the meal fills your belly. I use my dried three-onion mix, which is a combination of equal parts of yellow, red, and green onions, cut in ¼-inch pieces. This recipe is amenable to any substitutions and additions that please you: stew meat can be used to replace a roast; or instead of canned tomatoes, add more dried tomatoes and tomato juice. | Makes 4 to 8 servings.

- 2 pound beef roast • 1 quart canned tomatoes • 2 cups water • 1 cup dried tomatoes, cut in 1-inch pieces • ½ cup carrot slices • ¼ cup dried onion pieces • 1 tablespoon dried pepper pieces • 1 teaspoon dried basil, crushed • ½ teaspoon salt • ¼ teaspoon black pepper • ¼ teaspoon garlic

Cut away and discard as much of the fat and tissue from the meat as possible. Leave the bone in until the stew is done. Combine all ingredients in a slow cooker and cook until meat falls apart. On a high setting, it should be ready in 4 to 6 hours. If the liquid cooks away, simply add more. Serve over cooked potatoes.

Zucchini

One summer I was listening to a call-in talk radio show, and the host was asking for suggestions on how to deal with the prolific zucchini harvest. I could identify with this situation and chuckled at one caller's suggestion: "Find an unlocked parked car and fill it with zucchini." My solution, however, is to dry zucchini chips and make zucchini-rhubarb bread.

ZUCCHINI-RHUBARB BREAD

- ¾ cup dried shredded zucchini
- ½ cup dried rhubarb flakes • 1 ¼ cup water • 3 eggs • 1 cup butter, melted
- 2 cups sugar • 1 teaspoon vanilla
- ½ teaspoon cinnamon • ¼ teaspoon ground ginger • ¼ teaspoon ground cloves
- 2 ½ cups flour • 1 teaspoon baking powder • 1 teaspoon baking soda
- ½ teaspoon salt • 1 ½ cup nuts, chopped

Preheat oven to 325 degrees. Grease two 7-by-3-inch bread pans. In a small bowl, combine the zucchini, rhubarb, and water, stir, and let sit 30 minutes.

In a large bowl, beat eggs. Add butter, sugar, and vanilla and stir. Add rehydrated zucchini and rhubarb, cinnamon, ginger, and cloves. Stir again.

In another bowl, combine flour, baking powder, baking soda, and salt. Add to egg mixture and blend well. Add nuts. Stir. Divide batter into two pans. Let sit 15 minutes before baking to allow flavors to mingle. Bake 1 hour or until a toothpick comes out clean. Cool on wire racks.

ZUCCHINI CHIPS

Take torpedo zucchini, peel, cut in half, scoop out seeds, and slice into ⅛- to ¼-inch strips.

• ¼ cup soy sauce • 2 tablespoons water • 2 tablespoons rice vinegar • 1 heaping tablespoon garlic, roasted • 1 tablespoon sesame oil • 4 cups zucchini slices

Combine all ingredients, with the exception of zucchini, and blend. Add zucchini slices and marinate at least 1 hour before putting on mesh-lined dehydrator trays. Dry at 110 to 135 degrees until crisp.

> **Creative Idea** *Carefully layer colorful dried vegetables in pretty jars, tie a bow, and attach a recipe. Dried corn, dried green beans, dried onions, and dried tomatoes make a great soup base.*

TERIYAKI JERKY

BLOODY MARY JERKY

ROOT BEER JERKY

CAJUN JERKY

WINE JERKY

GROUND MEAT JERKY

TERIYAKI GROUND MEAT JERKY • JOE'S JERKY
SPICY TOMATO SOY JERKY • WHISKEY JERKY
HOT JERKY • TURKEY JERKY • HAM JERKY
SWEET HAM JERKY • UNFORGETTABLE SPAM JERKY

FISH JERKY

TROUT JERKY

JERKY AS AN INGREDIENT

JERKY BOUILLON • JERKY CAKE • JERKY ICE CREAM
TRADITIONAL PEMMICAN • MODERN PEMMICAN
JERKY PARFLECHES • JERKY BREAD
JERKY HASH • JERKY RICE
PASTA CON CARNE SECA

Jerky

Humans have benefited from eating dried meat since the Cro-Magnon era. Our ancestors learned about the natural drying process by observing and copying animals that cached their game in trees where it dried in the wind. Today, making jerky is the number one reason many people purchase a dehydrator.

Jerky Talk

Jerky is a popular low-carbohydrate, high-protein, low-fat snack and selling it is big business! In stores, a single-ounce can cost $2, making it more expensive than spiny lobster from the coldest waters of Maine.

Not only is jerky a tasty snack, it is also a great ingredient to use in baking and cooking. Outdoor enthusiasts have long known the benefit of adding jerky to a pot of soup.

Jerky is raw meat that is either:

- cut into ⅛- to ¼-inch thick strips that are marinated and then dried, or
- made with ground meat (like hamburger) that is flavored, shaped, and then dried.

Note that when I refer to meat, I'm including all categories: fish, poultry, or any other muscle meat. Some choices suitable for jerky include: beef, buffalo, venison, elk, moose, antelope, lamb, goat, chicken, turkey, duck, goose, ostrich, most fresh and saltwater fish, commercial luncheon meats, pepperoni, leftover cooked ham, cooked turkey, sausage, pastrami, and even tofu strips.

Jerky is considered raw meat. Since jerky is dried and not cooked, people always ask if jerky is safe to eat. The answer is yes, it is safe if it's been dried at a high enough temperature, long enough, and stored properly.

Although there is debate regarding the correct temperature to dry meat, the consensus is that it must be dried at a consistent temperature of at least 145 degrees and preferably 160 degrees. When drying precooked foods, such as ham, temperature is not as important. Meat needs to be dried at a higher temperature than fruits and vegetables because you must destroy the microorganisms that can survive at lower temperatures.

It's essential to be able to determine when jerky is dry. Water in meat must be removed, and the jerky must be dried enough so that it will not spoil. The time it takes to dry meat into jerky depends on the type of dehydrator, the amount of jerky you are making, water content, thickness of pieces, amount of humidity in the air, and the drying temperature.

Warm food always feels more pliable, so let jerky cool, then feel it in order to determine how dry it is. Squeeze a piece of dried jerky between your thumb and forefinger to detect moisture and soft spots. Finished jerky will bend like a green willow but is firm and will break when folded.

Although it is safer to over-dry than to under-dry, jerky that is dried too long or at too high a temperature becomes crisp and snaps clean like a dry stick.

One pound of raw meat will yield ⅓ to ½ pound of jerky. Strips 10 to 12 ¾ inches wide and 5 inches long that are dried at 160 degrees will generally dry in four to six hours. A round dehydrator tray that is 15½ inches across generally holds ¾ to 1 pound of ¼-inch thick strips.

Proper storage of jerky is also important. If your finished jerky feels oily, wrap it in paper towels to absorb the excess oil. This will help prevent rancidity and encourage longer storage. If the paper toweling gets saturated, discard it and wrap again with fresh paper towel.

I store jerky in sealable plastic bags or airtight jars with tight-fitting lids. Although our ancestors dried meat and fish and kept it from year to year without refrigeration, good packaging and cold temperatures promote longer shelf life. When I plan on keeping jerky longer than one month, I store it in the refrigerator or freezer. For a backpacking or camping trip, I package it in small, self-sealing plastic bags.

If jerky is not completely dried, mold can develop. If mold is found in a container of jerky, the entire contents must be discarded.

Making Strip Jerky

Making strip jerky can be as simple as sprinkling salt, pepper, and garlic on meat strips and then drying them. Although that is a valid way to make jerky, my goal is to introduce you to a bolder dimension in flavor blending. Jerky can be like fine wine, with a mingling of characteristics: some subtle, some robust. Imagine a sweet jerky that is a result of adding root beer to a marinade or a spicy tomato jerky that is excellent when paired with a vodka and tomato juice cocktail.

Start by choosing lean cuts of meat—such as flank, round, or loin—because they have less bone, connective tissue, and fat.

On a clean, flat cutting surface, use a sharp knife to remove excess fat, gristle, and any membranes and connective tissue. Eliminating as much fat as possible helps prevent jerky from turning rancid and reduces some of the gamey taste of wild meat.

Meat cut across the grain produces a jerky that is easier to break apart and chew. Cut ⅛- to ⅜-inch thick strips. Thin strips dry faster than thick ones.

Frozen or semi-frozen meat is easier to cut than meat that is at room temperature. An electric slicer is great way to cut semi-frozen meat into uniform-size strips that all dry in the same amount of time. Naturally thawed meat will have a better flavor and texture than meat thawed in a microwave.

Marinating

Marinades are seasoned liquids that can be as thick as molasses or water-thin. Marinating ingredients are mixed together and left for about fifteen minutes so that flavors have an opportunity to blend before adding strips.

The amount of time it will take strips to absorb flavoring can vary from a few minutes to several days. The longer the strips are in the marinade the more flavor they will absorb. Scoring meat allows a marinade to penetrate easier and

> **Caution:** *It is not a good idea to reuse a marinade because during the marinating process blood leaches into the marinating liquid.*

deeper. When marinating less than one hour, there is no need to refrigerate; but when marinating for more than one hour, cover the container and place it in the refrigerator. Big, thick strips will take longer for the marinade to penetrate. Make sure that all strips remain in contact with the flavorings, so stir or turn the strips at least once during the marinating process.

Once the strips are marinated, a colander can be used to drain the marinade off the strips. To dry, lay the flavored strips on a mesh-lined dehydrator tray with no overlapping of pieces so air can reach all surfaces. Dry at 160 degrees until the jerky bends like a green willow.

Flavoring Ingredients

There are endless combinations of flavoring ingredients to use when making a marinade. A marinade usually includes salt, an acid, a sweetener, herbs, and spices combined in various amounts. When concocting a marinade, smell, taste, and make adjustments before adding the meat.

Generally, 1 cup of marinade is used per 1 pound of strips.

Salt is the most common ingredient in a jerky marinade. Salt acts as a preservative and inhibits the growth of microorganisms that cause spoilage. Salt draws water and blood from the meat cells, induces partial drying, lengthens storage life, and adds flavor. Salt, or sodium chloride (NaCl), is essential to human life to maintain our equilibrium of liquids. A lack of salt increases the dangers of dehydration. Salt for marinades can be in the form of soy sauce, tamari, Tabasco, and Worcestershire sauce.

Sugar—white, brown, or maple sugars and honey, corn syrup, molasses, and artificial sweeteners add flavor and moderate the salt.

Oil does not dry, but small amounts of oil, such as olive and sesame, add flavor and enhance the texture of jerky.

Liquid smoke, especially hickory, is a popular flavoring. In my opinion, most people use too much liquid smoke and produce jerky that tastes like smoke and nothing else. However, when used in moderation, it can add a pleasing "campfire" flavor. Liquid smoke is made by burning sawdust, then condensing the smoke and separating out the carcinogenic tars, resins, and soot. Interestingly, it is safer to use liquid smoke than real smoke, and more convenient. Smoke, including liquid smoke, is a natural antioxidant, has an antibacterial effect, and serves as a preservative.

Herbs and **spices** add interest and flavor. Consider using both fresh and dried. Try adding basil, bay leaves, chervil, chives, dill, mint, oregano, parsley, rosemary, sage, savory, tarragon, or thyme. Some of my favorite spices are cardamom, cayenne, chili powder, cloves, coriander, cumin, curry, garlic, ginger, horseradish,

> **NOTE** *When puréeing any hot ingredients in a blender, cool before blending.*

juniper berries, mustard, nutmeg, paprika, and black, green, white, or pink peppercorns. Steep herbs like tea, strain, and add to marinades.

Use ⅛ to 1 teaspoon herbs or spices per 1 pound of meat.

Tenderizers help break down the cell structure of meat to make it more porous and tender. Piercing meat with a fork can help tenderizers penetrate deeper. Vinegar serves as a tenderizing agent and helps meat reach its lowest water holding capacity so that it dries faster.

Alcohol and jerky flatter each other. I understand how jerky and beer became good companions. Beer, wine, vodka, and whiskey. add flavor and have a tenderizing effect, but the alcohol itself evaporates when used in jerky. I concentrate and release the flavor of alcohol by simmering it about ten minutes. Use a high-sided pan to minimize the chance of it catching on fire; however, if it does flame, the flame will die when the alcohol is gone. One cup of alcohol reduces to about ¼ cup.

Use ¼ cup beer, wine, or liquor per 1 pound of meat.

Fruits and **vegetables** can be juiced, puréed, grated, minced, chopped, and added to marinades. Consider using lemon, orange, pineapple, apple, or tomato juice. Minced cooked onions add a rich sweetness to a marinade. Try adding celery, garlic, papaya, and horseradish powder.

Use 1 teaspoon fruit or vegetable to ¼ cup per 1 pound of meat.

Use 1 teaspoon salt per 1 pound of meat.
Use 1 teaspoon to 1 tablespoon sugar per 1 pound of meat.
Use 1 tablespoon oil per 1 pound of meat.
Use ½ teaspoon liquid smoke per 1 pound of meat.
Use ¼ cup vinegar per 1 pound of meal.

Marinating Containers

Earthenware crocks, glass bowls, and self-sealing plastic bags make good marinating containers. Plastic bags take up less space than bowls and make cleanup easy. By squeezing any excess air out of the bag, you can force the marinade into the strips. When using bowls or other containers, stir the strips every couple of hours to make sure the marinade is able to penetrate all the strips.

Smart Labeling

1. Use a waterproof pen to write the type of jerky and the drying date on a piece of masking tape.
2. Place this tape on the marinating container.
3. When done marinating, transfer this same label to the drying trays.
4. When the jerky is dry, place this same label on the storage container.

Marinating Options

Vacuum It

If you have a vacuum packer, place the strips and the marinade in the special vacuum bags or in a canning jar (jars are best), and pull a vacuum. The vacuum will force the marinade throughout the cell tissues and help shorten the marinating time.

Brush It

After the marinated strips have been placed on mesh-lined dehydrator trays and dried for an hour or so and the surface moisture has evaporated, you can intensify the flavor by dipping a brush into a bowl of molasses, honey, or barbecue sauce. Apply a thin coating to the surface of the meat, then continue the drying process.

Spray It

Fill a spray atomizer with a thin marinade and spray the top and bottom of the drying strips as many times as you like during the drying process. Try using a little teriyaki sauce and fresh garlic that's been twirled in a blender.

Do the Double-Dip

If the finished jerky is dried too hard or crisp, or has too little flavor, or it's simply a failure and you'd rather fix it than throw it away, try the double-dip trick. All you have to do is soak your rejected jerky for 10 minutes in another marinade and then dry it again. Not only has this rescued my failed jerky, it has resulted in some very tasty creations.

> NOTE *Make small batches the first couple of times you make jerky. Then, over time, tweak your recipes to satisfy your palate and gradually make larger quantities. Keep notes on the recipes you like, what you don't like, and the adjustments you want for the next batch. Include weight of fresh meat, flavoring changes, and how long it was marinated. Jerky making may turn into your most creative culinary expression.*

Do the Two-Step

Marinate any meat strips in whatever marinade you like. Drain and lay on mesh-lined dehydrator trays, but dry only half way. Remove the drying strips and soak again in a marinade for at least one hour, drain, and finish the drying process.

TERIYAKI JERKY

This popular jerky should maybe be called "Everybody Likes This Jerky." The following two recipes are basically the same but with different quantities of meat strips to give you an idea of how to adjust ingredients when increasing poundage. Over the years we have all agreed that this family favorite is best when marinated at least 12 hours.

For 1 pound meat strips • ⅔ cup teriyaki sauce • 1 teaspoon brown sugar • 1 teaspoon olive oil • 1 teaspoon garlic, minced • ½ teaspoon fresh ginger, finely grated • ¼ teaspoon black pepper, coarsely ground • ¼ teaspoon salt • ¼ teaspoon liquid smoke

For 5 pounds meat strips • 3 cups teriyaki sauce • 2 tablespoons olive oil • 2 heaping tablespoons brown sugar • 1 heaping tablespoon garlic, mined • 1 tablespoon black pepper, coarsely ground • 1 tablespoon salt • 1 tablespoon liquid smoke • 1 tablespoon fresh ginger, finely grated

In a bowl, combine all the ingredients except the strips and stir until well blended. Add meat and stir with a sturdy fork. Marinate at least 1 hour. When marinating longer, place in the refrigerator. Drain in a colander. Place strips on a mesh-lined dehydrator tray and dry at a minimum temperature of 145 degrees to 160 degrees. To check for doneness, first turn the dehydrator off and let the jerky cool, then feel it to determine if it is dry.

BLOODY MARY JERKY

Chew on this jerky or add a handful of small pieces to spaghetti sauce.

For 1 pound strips • ½ cup V8 • ⅓ cup vodka • 1 tablespoon Worcestershire sauce • 1 teaspoon honey • 1 teaspoon lemon juice • 1 teaspoon celery salt • ½ teaspoon hot sauce • ½ teaspoon fresh horseradish, grated • ½ teaspoon black pepper, ground

In a bowl, combine all the ingredients except the strips and stir until well blended. Add meat and stir with a sturdy fork. Marinate at least 1 hour. When marinating longer, place in the refrigerator. Drain in a colander. Place strips on a mesh-lined dehydrator tray and dry at a minimum temperature of 145 degrees to 160 degrees.

ROOT BEER JERKY

This sweet and tangy marinade works well with wild meats.

For 1 pound strips • 3 cups root beer • 1 tablespoon garlic, minced • 1 teaspoon black pepper • 1 teaspoon salt • 1 teaspoon liquid smoke • ¼ teaspoon pepper

Over medium heat, reduce root beer to 1 cup. Remove from heat and add all remaining ingredients. Let strips marinate at least 1 hour. When marinating longer, place in the refrigerator. Drain in a colander, place on a mesh-lined dehydrator tray, and sprinkle the top of the strips with a little salt. Dry at a minimum temperature of 145 degrees to 160 degrees.

CAJUN JERKY

$\mathbf{A}$dd zip to this marinade by adding more cayenne pepper, and if still not hot enough, add finely chopped jalapeño or habanero peppers.

For 1 pound strips • 1 cup tomato juice • 2 teaspoons cayenne pepper • 1 ½ teaspoons dried thyme • 1 ½ teaspoons dried basil • 1 ½ teaspoons onion powder • 1 teaspoon white pepper • ½ teaspoon black pepper • ½ teaspoon garlic powder

In a bowl, combine all ingredients except strips and stir until well blended. Add meat and stir with a sturdy fork. Marinate at least 1 hour. When marinating longer, place in the refrigerator. Drain in a colander. Place strips on a mesh-lined dehydrator tray and dry at a minimum temperature of 145 degrees to 160 degrees.

WINE JERKY

For 1 pound strips • 1 cup Burgundy wine • ¼ cup soy sauce • 2 tablespoons molasses • 1 tablespoon garlic, chopped • 1 tablespoon olive oil • 1 tablespoon black pepper, coarsely ground

In a bowl, combine all the ingredients except the strips and stir until well blended. Add meat and stir with a sturdy fork. Marinate at least 1 hour. When marinating longer, place in the refrigerator. Drain in a colander. Place strips on a mesh-lined dehydrator tray and dry at a minimum temperature of 145 degrees to 160 degrees.

GROUND MEAT JERKY

$\mathbf{M}$aking jerky out of ground meat has advantages over making it from strips of meat. Ground meat jerky:

- Tastes great
- Is cheaper to make than strip jerky

- Takes less time to make than strip jerky
- Can be made by combining various meats— like half venison and half beef
- Uses all of the meat—there are no leftover scraps like when making strip jerky
- Does not waste flavorings or marinades, because it is all absorbed in the meat
- Dries uniformly because all pieces are the same size
- Dries faster than strip jerky
- Can be made in different shapes, like bears or cows
- Is easier to chew
- Is easy and fun to make!

> *Did you know that half of commercially processed venison is made into venison jerky or sausage? Processing a medium-sized deer can cost over $100.*

My husband Joe hunts, and we make jerky to give away as Christmas presents. Plus, during the hunting season, friends and family give us their venison to make into jerky. We find that using commercial flavorings along with a few added ingredients is a very easy way to process a lot of meat. Joe likes to combine half venison and half beef, or half venison and half buffalo, because venison alone can be too lean. A little fat will give meat more flavor and better texture. Sometimes we sprinkle the top of the wet jerky with a little salt and pepper.

Seasoning Ground Meat

The same marinating ingredients can be used with strip and ground meat jerky. The difference is that all of the marinade is absorbed when added to ground meat; therefore, use no more than ½ cup of liquid with 1 pound of ground meat.

Once flavorings are added to ground meat, allow at least 15 minutes for all the ingredients to blend before shaping it into jerky.

> *When thawing frozen ground meat, break up any clumps larger than ¼ inch so the flavorings can penetrate. Large clumps can jam up extruding devices.*

Shaping Ground Meat

After the ground meat is flavored, it needs to be forced into a shape. One pound of ground meat will make between ten and twelve strips, each ¾ inch wide and 5 inches long.

Take Aim with a Jerky Gun

"Jerky guns" or "jerky shooters" are devices used to extrude ground meat into uniformly sized pieces. These gadgets look like caulk guns or cake decorators and have various shaped nozzles for making jerky into strips or sticks. Jerky guns are generally available from dehydrator manufacturers or catalogs that sell to hunters and fisher-people. To use, fill the chamber or barrel with the flavored ground meat, then pull the trigger to force the meat into uniform pieces.

Handmade

Meat mixtures are easier to handle if your hands are wet and the mixture is cold.

The longer you mix the ground meat mixture the better the finished jerky will hold together. With your hands, shape the flavored ground meat into 1-inch balls. Place each ball on top of a piece of plastic wrap or waxed paper. Cover with another piece of wrap or paper. With a rolling pin, flatten the balls into ⅛- to ¼-inch rounds that are about 2 inches in diameter. Uniform thickness is necessary so the jerky dries evenly. If the center of the patty jerky is not completely dry, the jerky can mold.

Fun Jerky

Spread a sheet of wax paper on your kitchen counter. Spoon the flavored meat mixture on the wax paper. Lay another sheet of wax paper on top of the mixture. With a rolling pin, flatten the meat to ¼ inch thick. Press animal shaped cookie cutters down firmly to make deep impressions. Choose a deer shaped cutter for ground venison and a cow shape for ground beef.

Carefully remove the shaped mixture and place on top of a lightly oiled leather sheet. Dry at 155 degrees until it firms up. Remove the drying jerky from the sheet and place on a mesh-lined dehydrator tray to make it easier for dry air to get to it. Return to the dehydrator and complete the drying process. When checking for doneness, make sure the center is completely dry.

Gun-less Jerky

Spoon the flavored ground meat mixture on to a leather sheet. With a large spoon, a greased rolling pin, or the palm of your hand, spread and evenly flatten the mixture. Place the meat-filled leather sheet in a dehydrator and dry at 155 degrees, long enough so the meat can be cut and still hold its shape (usually 1 to 2 hours). Use a pizza cutter or a serrated knife to make indentations or cut lines 1 to 1 ½ inches apart in the drying meat. Return the tray to the dehydrator and dry until the strips can be broken apart at the cut lines. Remove the strips from the leather sheets and place on a mesh-lined dehydrator tray so air can easily move around the jerky and the meat can finish drying.

Family Fun

This is another way to shape meat and make jerky. I learned this technique from a Boy Scout dad. While I was packing up after a presentation to a Scout troop about why food drying is great for outdoor adventuring, one

of the dads offered to help me schlep my stuff to my van. He said, "I'd like to share an idea with you." Then he told me how his whole family participated in making ground meat jerky. "We homeschool our kids and we like to approach life in a creative way," he said. "We use a Play-Doh Fun Factory to shape our jerky," he chuckled. "It's fun to make jerky in all those shapes. Try it!" he encouraged.

TERIYAKI GROUND MEAT JERKY

This recipe is very similar to the Teriyaki Jerky on page 77. Since this recipe uses ground meat, the quantity of liquid is reduced. Too much liquid in a ground meat marinade can make the finished jerky crumble and fall apart.

For 1 pound ground meat • ⅓ cup teriyaki sauce • 1 teaspoon brown sugar • 1 teaspoon olive oil • 1 teaspoon garlic, minced • 1 teaspoon black pepper, coarsely ground • ½ teaspoon fresh ginger, finely grated • ¼ teaspoon salt • ¼ teaspoon liquid smoke

For 5 pounds ground meat • 2 cups teriyaki sauce • 2 tablespoons olive oil • 2 heaping tablespoons brown sugar • 1 heaping tablespoon garlic, mined • 1 heaping tablespoon black pepper, coarsely ground • 1 tablespoon salt • 1 tablespoon liquid smoke • 1 tablespoon fresh ginger, finely grated

In a bowl, combine all the ingredients except the ground meat, and stir until blended. Let the ingredients blend at least 15 minutes. Add meat, and stir with a sturdy fork or by hand. Marinate at least 1 hour. If marinating longer, place in the refrigerator. Form into shapes and place on a mesh-lined dehydrator tray. Dry at a minimum temperature of 145 degrees to 160 degrees. To check for doneness, first turn the dehydrator off and let the jerky cool, then feel it to determine if it is dry.

JOE'S JERKY

Commercially prepared spice mixtures can be used with other ingredients to make terrific jerky. For over thirty years I have done business with the NESCO/American Harvest dehydrator company and as a result I have the most experience with their line of spices. Please feel free to substitute your favorite spices for those mentioned in my recipes.

For 5 pounds ground meat • 2 packages Nesco's original spice • 1 package Nesco's pepperoni spice • 1 cup soy sauce • 2 tablespoons olive oil • 2 tablespoons brown sugar • 1 tablespoon garlic powder • ½ teaspoon black pepper

For 10 pounds ground meat • 3 packages Nesco's original spice • 3 packages Nesco's hot and spicy spice • 3 cups soy sauce • ⅔ cup brown sugar • ¼ cup olive oil • 3 tablespoons garlic • 2 tablespoons pepper

In a bowl, combine all the ingredients except the ground meat, and stir until blended. Let the mixture sit at least 15 minutes. Add meat and stir with a sturdy fork. Marinate at least 1 hour. If marinating longer, place in the refrigerator. Form into shapes and place on a mesh-lined dehydrator tray. Dry at a minimum temperature of 145 to 160 degrees.

SPICY TOMATO SOY JERKY

For 1 pound ground meat • ⅓ cup tomato sauce • 3 tablespoons soy sauce • 2 tablespoons Worcestershire sauce • 1 tablespoon brown sugar • ½ teaspoon garlic powder • ½ teaspoon black pepper, freshly ground • ½ teaspoon horseradish, freshly grated • ½ teaspoon Tabasco • ½ teaspoon liquid smoke • ½ teaspoon salt

Put all ingredients, with the exception of meat, in a blender. Put ground meat in a bowl, add blended ingredients, mix, and marinate at least 1 hour. If marinating longer, place in the refrigerator. Form into shapes and place on a mesh-lined dehydrator tray. Dry at a minimum temperature of 145 to 160 degrees.

WHISKEY JERKY

What could be better than booze and a hunk of meat all in one bite? Vary the booze; try rum, scotch, and brandy. Once the meat is dry, add more flavor by dipping the jerky in whiskey and drying again.

For 1 pound ground meat • 2 cups cheap whiskey • 1 tablespoon soy sauce • 1 tablespoon brown sugar • 1 tablespoon olive oil • 1 teaspoon salt • ½ teaspoon liquid smoke • ½ teaspoon garlic, minced • ¼ teaspoon black peppercorns, crushed

Reduce whiskey to ⅓ cup in a pan with high sides to prevent the fumes from flaming. Be careful. If a flame does appear, it will subside when the alcohol is gone. Cool and then add remaining ingredients to the whiskey; stir; then add ground meat. Marinate at least 1 hour. If marinating longer, place in the refrigerator. Form into shapes and place on a mesh-lined dehydrator tray. Dry at a minimum temperature of 145 to 160 degrees.

HOT JERKY

If you want your upper lip to sweat, use habanero peppers.

For 1 pound ground meat • ⅓ cup teriyaki sauce
• 2 tablespoons hot peppers, seeded and finely chopped • 1 tablespoon olive oil • 1 tablespoon minced garlic • 2 teaspoons brown sugar
• 1 teaspoon black pepper, freshly ground
• 1 teaspoon horseradish, freshly grated
• 1 teaspoon salt • ½ teaspoon paprika • ½ teaspoon chili powder • ½ teaspoon Tabasco

In a bowl, combine all the ingredients except the ground meat, and stir until blended. Let the mixture sit at least 15 minutes. Add meat and stir with a sturdy fork. Marinate at least 1 hour. If marinating longer, place in the refrigerator. Form into shapes and place on a mesh-lined dehydrator tray. Dry at a minimum temperature of 145 to 160 degrees.

TURKEY JERKY

People like saying "Turkey Jerky," and then after they try it they usually smack their lips with delight.

For 1 pound ground meat • 2 tablespoons lemon juice • 2 tablespoons onion, freshly grated • 2 tablespoons teriyaki sauce • 1 tablespoon white sugar • 1 tablespoon olive oil • 1 tablespoon lemon peel, fresh grated • 2 teaspoons paprika • 1 teaspoon garlic, crushed • 1 teaspoon salt • 1 teaspoon black pepper, freshly ground • ½ teaspoon liquid smoke
• ¼ teaspoon Tabasco • 1 pound ground turkey • Salt, to sprinkle

In a bowl, combine all the ingredients except the ground meat and stir until blended. Let the mixture rest at least 15 minutes. Add meat and stir with a sturdy fork. Marinate at least 1 hour. If marinating longer, place in the refrigerator. Form into shapes and place on a mesh-lined dehydrator tray. Sprinkle salt on the jerky while it's still moist. Dry at a minimum temperature of 145 to 160 degrees.

Ham Jerky

For 1 pound ham slices • ¼ cup honey • 2 teaspoons Dijon mustard • 2 teaspoons dried pink peppercorns, crushed • 2 teaspoons dried green peppercorns, crushed • ½ teaspoon black peppercorns, coarsely ground • Mix all ingredients together, wait 15 minutes and then add ham slices. Marinate at least 12 hours before drying on mesh-lined dehydrator trays at 145 degrees.

Our friend Judy Lynch specializes in conducting horse pack trips throughout North America. After one trip to the Bob Marshall Wilderness in Montana she was discouraged by the response to the trail food she had provided. "I didn't know if I'd ever be able to go on another pack trip unless somehow it got easier," she recalls. Judy loves to cook and takes pride in serving good food. "I want everyone to smack their lips and say, 'WOW! That meal was incredible!'" Judy attended a food drying class and afterward dried all the food necessary for a five-day pack trip. "Drying food was the key," she said happily. "I experienced less stress, my food budget was reduced, the horses packed lighter loads (all the food supplies fit in one large duffel bag), and everyone loved the food, including my husband, who enjoys traditional home cooking." She paused, "Dan said it was the best trail food he'd ever eaten. Ham jerky was the biggest hit. Everybody loved it." She continued, "Riders always want something salty to snack on, and the ham jerky satisfied that desire. Bringing chips on a pack trip is not an easy task, and it's a good idea to eat something salty because it makes the riders drink more water. I also liked that it was different." Choose cooked lean ham slices for jerky and cut ¼ inch thick. Making ham jerky can be as easy as mixing mustard and honey together, painting the ham slices, and then drying. Ham jerky is also a great addition to any split pea soup.

SWEET HAM JERKY

For a twist, you can substitute maple syrup or brown sugar for the honey in this recipe and sprinkle a little black pepper on the slices right after laying them on the mesh-lined dehydrator tray.

For 1 pound ham strips • ²/₃ cup frozen orange juice concentrate • ½ cup honey • ¹/₃ cup whiskey • 1 teaspoon black pepper, freshly ground

Mix all ingredients together, wait 15 minutes, and then add ham strips. Marinate at least 12 hours before drying. Place on a mesh-lined dehydrator tray and dry at 145 degrees.

UNFORGETTABLE SPAM JERKY

I was puzzled one day when I received in my mailbox a brown envelope with no return address. Inside there was a sheet of white paper with the words "Unforgettable Spam Jerky." There was no signature. This sparked my curiosity, so I went to the store for a can of Spam Luncheon Meat. After it dried, the result was a jerky that tasted very similar to the jerky you can buy at a convenience store.

- 1 12-ounce can of Spam • 3 tablespoons soy sauce • 3 tablespoons water
- 2 tablespoons brown sugar • 1 teaspoon Worcestershire sauce • ¼ teaspoon fresh horseradish, grated • ¼ teaspoon chili powder • ¼ teaspoon liquid smoke

Remove Spam from the can and cut into 12 even slices. Pile slices on top of each other, make two more cuts through the slices for a total of 36 pieces.

Combine all the other ingredients in a sealable plastic bag. Swish around and then add the slices. Marinate at least 12 hours in the refrigerator. Because Spam is precooked it can be dried at any temperature. Dry until chewy, not crunchy.

FISH JERKY

Fish is more delicate than meat, absorbs flavor more easily, and dries faster. To dry fish, first rinse them in fresh, clean, cool water. Fillet and cut into thin strips about ¼-inch thick, ½-inch wide, and 3 to 4 inches long. Slashing cuts made crosswise in the flesh will help flavorings penetrate.

One of the most fascinating things I've found while researching dried foods is that almost every kind of fish has been dried throughout time in almost every corner of the world, despite fish being a relatively difficult food to preserve.

With more than 20,000 species, fish is often referred to as "wheat of the sea." It has been dried and used as a principal food source and survival insurance throughout the world. Historically, fish was coated heavily with salt, dried in the sun and wind, hung over fires and smoked, strung on hooks, suspended from poles, and laid on bamboo racks and hot flat rocks. Most fish dried in this way was used as protein in cooking and not eaten as fish jerky.

TROUT JERKY

I remember the day my husband got lucky and landed an 18-inch brown trout. I turned it into jerky and left it in the dehydrator to cool. When I went to put it away, it was completely gone. My husband ate it all before one piece ever made it into a storage container. I **One pound of fresh fish will generally dry to ⅓ pound.**

For 1 pound fish strips • ¼ cup soy sauce • 1 teaspoon olive oil • 1 teaspoon sesame oil • 1 teaspoon sugar
• 1 teaspoon lemon juice • 1 teaspoon minced garlic • ¼ teaspoon salt
• ¼ teaspoon black pepper, freshly ground

In a bowl, combine all the ingredients except the strips and stir until blended. Allow mixture to rest for 15 minutes. Add strips and stir with a

sturdy fork. Marinate at least 1 hour. When marinating longer, place in the refrigerator. Drain in a colander and place on a mesh-lined dehydrator tray and dry at a minimum temperature of 145 to 160 degrees.

Jerky as an Ingredient

Few people know that jerky is a flavorful, delicious, interesting, even outrageous recipe ingredient. I've often wondered why jerky companies do not add that possibility to their labeling and advertising. Think about adding small pieces of jerky to soup, stew, hash, spaghetti sauce, casseroles, rice, and pasta dishes. Use crumpled jerky just like commercial bacon bits on salads or in omelets. Try substituting small pieces of jerky for pepperoni or sprinkle it on top of a pizza. Native Americans are known to have added jerky to pots of dried corn, squash, and beans.

When adding jerky to a dish that has adequate liquids, such as a soup or stew, there is no need to presoak or rehydrate. When rehydration is necessary, consider soaking jerky in wine, vegetable and fruit juices, even liquor. Instead of discarding any excess rehydrating liquid, try to combine it in the recipe. One cup of jerky soaked in 1 cup of liquid results in about 1½ cups of rehydrated jerky.

> A slow cooker is a great appliance for rehydrating and cooking jerky.

The smaller the piece of jerky, the faster it will rehydrate. Depending on the size of jerky pieces, rehydrating time can vary from just a few minutes to an hour. When rehydrating takes longer than one hour, put the jerky in the refrigerator. Generally ½-inch pieces will rehydrate in about 15 minutes. Warmer liquids shorten the rehydration time.

JERKY BOUILLON

Native Americans ground jerky by using a rock mortar and pestle. They mixed the powdered jerky with hot water to make a coffee-like drink. Cut jerky with kitchen shears into ½-inch pieces. Grind in a blender, ¼ cup at a time. One strip of jerky that is 1 inch wide and 5 inches long will grind to 1 tablespoon of powder. | Makes 1 cup.

- ⅓ cup powdered jerky • 1 cup water

Mix jerky and water together. Allow 5 to 10 minutes to rehydrate. Boiling water will promote faster rehydration. Uncooked, rehydrated jerky must be refrigerated if not used within one hour.

JERKY CAKE

This recipe was prompted by an elegant meal at a very fancy restaurant where dessert was pepper ice cream. As we discussed this strange blend of ingredients, I said I could top it and went home and baked my first jerky cake. Although we were a little dubious about the first bite, surprisingly, we all thought it was a hoot and worth the effort. | Makes 12 servings.

- 1 box (16.75 ounces) 1-step angel food cake mix • ½ cup dried jerky powder

Make angel food cake according to instructions on box. After the cake is completely blended, fold in the jerky powder. Stir only enough to mix thoroughly. Bake according to box directions. Cake should cool before frosting.

Follow directions on frosting box. Once frosting is completely mixed, add powdered jerky. Frost cake and dribble shredded jerky over the top, like you would chocolate or coconut.

Place ice cream in a large container with a tight-fitting lid. Use a knife to cut the ice cream into small pieces. Add jerky and pepper and mix. Cover the container and place in freezer. Serve in small tablespoon dollops with jerky cake.

Jerky Frosting • *1 package (7.2 ounces) fluffy white frosting* • *2 tablespoons jerky, powdered* • *1 teaspoon jerky, shredded*

Jerky Ice Cream • *1 pint vanilla ice cream* • *2 tablespoons powdered jerky* • *½ teaspoon black peppercorns, finely ground*

Traditional Pemmican

Pemmican is one of the earliest and most important high-protein, portable foods. Not only did pemmican nourish the Native Americans, it also served as a compact staple food for the pioneers in their westward ventures. Pemmican is a combination of powdered or finely chopped dried meat, dried berries, and melted animal fat that is mixed into a thick paste and stuffed into airtight animal skins. Dried wild fruits such as strawberries, blueberries, huckleberries, raspberries, cherries, buffalo berries, grapes (raisins), and plums were pounded into a chunky powder. Cracked bones were boiled in water and the rich, sweet, salty butter-like fat was skimmed off and added to pemmican, as was animal fat that was cut into small (1-inch) chunks and heated in a pan over a slow fire. To store pemmican, casings from animal innards (intestines and stomach linings) were scraped clean and stuffed with the meat, fat, and dried fruit mixture.

MODERN PEMMICAN

This pemmican can be made using either strips or ground meat jerky. Feel free to vary the ingredients. Add a pinch of ground red pepper, chopped peanuts, a touch of honey, and dried apricots, apples, peaches, prunes, pineapple, kiwi, raisins, and strawberries. If you add dried rose hips (vitamin C) you will get an almost completely life-sustaining portable food.

• 1 ½ cup powdered jerky • 1 cup dried fruit, chopped in ⅛-inch pieces • 1 cup peanut butter • Plastic wrap

Grind a few small pieces of jerky at a time in the blender or food processor, set aside, and then grind the dried fruits. Combine all ingredients and mix well. Spread a 12-by-14-inch sheet of plastic wrap flat on the counter. Spoon half the mixture onto the wrap and form a log shape. Firmly pull the wrap around the pemmican mixture to force and compress it. Repeat with the other half of the mixture. Make sure it's wrapped well to keep air out. Store in the refrigerator until you leave for an outdoor adventure where it can be carried in a pack; up to one month or so.

JERKY PARFLECHES

As you are dining on this fancy dish, think back to the time when wild buffalo roamed the land and people regularly dried their food. | Makes 4 servings.

- 1 cup jerky, coarsely chopped • 1 cup dried cranberries, coarsely chopped
  • ¼ cup butter, melted • ¾ cup dried wild plums, coarsely chopped • ¾ cup
  dried cherries, coarsely chopped • 1 ½ tablespoons red wine vinegar •
  1 tablespoon fresh thyme, finely chopped • 1 tablespoon fresh rosemary,
  finely chopped • ¼ cup frozen orange juice concentrate, thawed •
  ¼ cup butter, melted • 30 sheets (12 by 17 inches each) phyllo
  dough • 2 cups butter, melted • 1 cup breadcrumbs

Combine all but last 3 ingredients and stir. Set aside and allow time for the ingredients to moisten. Place one phyllo sheet on a clean, dry work surface. Brush a light layer of butter, starting with the edges and covering the entire surface. Sprinkle a pinch of breadcrumbs over the sheet. Crumbs serve to ensure the phyllo dough remains flaky between each layer. Use 5 sheets phyllo dough to build 5 layers in this manner. Cut this stack into 4 pieces, 6 inches wide and 8 ½ inches long. Place one rounded tablespoon of jerky mixture in the center of each square and fold phyllo edges into the center to form a "purse." Use melted butter to bind the dough together. Repeat this process with remaining phyllo sheets. Place on a cookie sheet and bake 15 to 20 minutes at 400 degrees until golden.

Mix orange juice and honey together and drizzle over the parfleches while they are still warm.

Topping
- $\frac{2}{3}$ cup frozen orange juice concentrate, thawed
- $\frac{1}{3}$ cup honey

JERKY BREAD

An entire meal can be packed inside a loaf of bread.

• 1 loaf raw bread dough • ½ cup jerky, chopped into ¼-inch pieces • 3 tablespoons water • 1 tablespoon dried tomato pieces • 1 tablespoon dried onion pieces • 1 teaspoon black pepper, finely ground

In a small bowl combine all ingredients except dough. Let the ingredients sit at least 15 minutes. Knead the rehydrated ingredients into dough. Place dough in an oiled baking tin and bake at 350 degrees. When the crust browns, remove from oven, spread butter on top, and set the loaf on its side to cool.

JERKY HASH

This is a great way to use leftover baked potatoes. | Makes 4 servings.

- ½ cup jerky, cut in ½-inch pieces
- ¼ cup water • ½ cup celery, chopped
- 3 green onions, chopped • ½ teaspoon garlic, minced • 1 tablespoon olive oil
- 3 cups leftover baked potatoes, cubed • Salt • Pepper

In a bowl, rehydrate jerky in water 10 minutes. Drain and save jerky-flavored water. Over high heat, sauté celery, oil, and onion and reduce heat to medium. Add saved jerky water, cover, and cook. Remove lid and add potatoes, jerky, salt, and pepper. Stir to prevent sticking.

JERKY RICE

Makes 4 servings.

• 1 cup short-grain brown rice • ¼ cup jerky, cut in ¼-inch pieces • 2 tablespoons dried tomato pieces, broken in ¼-inch pieces • 1 tablespoon olive oil • ¼ teaspoon dried basil • ¼ teaspoon dried oregano • 2 ¼ cups water

Jerky is a wonderful base for making rice and veggies. Just add small pieces of fresh vegetables for crunch, such as bell pepper and carrots.

Combine all ingredients and simmer uncovered 20 to 30 minutes.

PASTA CON CARNE SECA

This is an elegant, yet simple, rich, and pretty dish that works really well with wild meat jerky. | Makes 2 servings.

- 1 cup jerky, cut in ¼-inch pieces
- 1 cup white wine • ½ cup half dried mushroom pieces • ½ cup dried pepper pieces • ¼ cup dried tomato pieces • 3 tablespoons butter • 1 cup whipping cream • 1 teaspoon basil, finely chopped • 1 cup thin pasta • ½ cup Parmesan cheese • ⅛ teaspoon black pepper, coarsely ground

Put jerky and wine in a saucepan and let sit for 15 minutes. Bring to a simmer, add mushrooms, pepper, and tomato pieces and cook until wine disappears. Reduce to low heat, add butter and add cream. Stir until thick. Prepare pasta according to directions, then drain and add to jerky mixture. Add basil. Serve over the cooked pasta and top with cheese and pepper.

DRIED SPAGHETTI SAUCE

THE ULTIMATE TRAIL MIX

JUDY'S "WOW" HAM CURRY

VEGETABLE SOUP

COOKED GROUND MEAT

GOULASH

Food for the Adventurer

Lightweight Snacks

Outdoor enthusiasts sing the praises of lightweight dried foods. No reasonable backpacker is going to lug a 25-ounce jar of spaghetti sauce up a mountain. Instead, he will dry that jar of spaghetti sauce down to about 3 ounces. Once dry, he will fit it in a small plastic bag, add some dried spaghetti and dried Parmesan cheese, and take it along to rehydrate and enjoy any time and any place.

Quick and simple meals can be made more satisfying with the addition of dried fruits, vegetables, meat, and spices. Dried split pea or lentil soup seasoned with curry and served over rice and beans becomes an exotic meal. When camping, spiff up prepackaged macaroni and cheese with a handful of crushed dried tomatoes. Make tacos by rehydrating dried ground meat, dried refried beans, dried spinach, and dried salsa and serve in warmed tortilla shells.

One summer I put my experiments to the test on a 5-day trip into the Rocky Mountains. The total weight of enough food to feed two people was 10 pounds and I'm proud to say we ate like royalty. Breakfasts were simple, mainly oatmeal or granola and tea or coffee. For lunch we snacked on jerky, dried fruits, and nuts. Our evening meals were fabulous. We dined on homemade vegetable soup, ham curry, spaghetti sauce with hamburger, and goulash. Our grand finale at the top of a mountain was tacos. We capped off our evening meals by adding dried fruit powders to various flavors of pudding.

Develop your menu after you know how many people are going on the trip and tally up the number of meals you'll need. If possible, determine what everyone likes and dislikes, and take note of any special dietary needs. It is best to maintain a diet that is as normal as possible. People generally have hearty appetites when traveling in the out-of-doors, so it's a good idea to bring more food than you think you'll need (without going overboard).

Thinking ahead can make the difference between having a terrific time or a terrible experience when hiking. Planning and preparing lightweight, portable meals takes time and forethought. Although it's work, it is always a good idea to test any new recipe at home before trying it on the trail.

Keep a list from one trip to the next to save time and prevent something important from being left at home.

Food	Starting Weight	Dried Weight
Canned pineapple rings	20 ounces	3 ounces
Fresh tomatoes	16 ounces	1 ounce
Frozen vegetables	30 ounces	4 ounces
Canned fruit cocktail	21 ounces	3 ounces
Canned cream soup	13 ounces	2 ounces
Canned water-packed tuna	6 ounces	1 ounce
Spaghetti sauce	25 ounces	3 ounces
Cooked ground meat	16 ounces	5 ounces
Meat strips for making jerky	16 ounces	6 ounces

Packaging

Outdoors people employ various packaging styles. Some put all breakfasts in one bag, lunches in another, and dinners in yet another. Some pack each food item separately and stuff everything in one large duffel bag. Others keep the food they'll need for each day in separate bags. Whatever your preference, label all bags and include any preparation instructions or directions.

A utility bag contains beverages and individual condiments, such as sugar, cream containers, salt, pepper, little packets of peanut butter, mayonnaise, mustard, ketchup, jelly, honey, salad dressing, and cream cheese obtained from grocery stores or fast-food establishments, plus cooking and eating utensils. An empty 35mm film can makes a handy dried herb storage container. Remember to label the container because dried herbs can be difficult to distinguish from one another. To avoid over-packing, once you have all your stuff ready put it in a pile, go through it again, and think ahead in order to eliminate any unnecessary items.

Pack fresh bread, crackers, and cookies carefully to avoid crushing. Select hearty whole grain breads, bagels, tortillas, English muffins, and pita bread because they do not crush as easily. Most cheese contains oil and in warm weather, it breaks down and becomes runny. Take along hard cheeses, like Romano, Parmesan, Asiago, and dry Jack. Package all liquids, such as oil, in lightweight, leak-proof, sturdy, and conveniently shaped plastic tubes or bottles. Fresh carrots, cabbage, onions, and cucumbers travel well, plus add crunch and flavor to meals. Lemons and oranges travel well, but most other fresh fruits bruise too easily. Repack any store-bought prepared foods in self-sealing plastic bags and include any preparation directions.

How About Rehydrating? *An hour or so before you want to eat, put dried food and a little water in a container, then heat the plumped-up food and serve. Recycled plastic peanut butter jars with tight-fitting lids make great rehydration containers.*

While in camp, consider filling a thermos with hot water. Then anytime during the day you can easily make a quick cup of hot tea, coffee, or instant soup. At night, put steel-cut oats, dried fruit pieces, hot water, and a little sugar in a thermos—in the morning breakfast will be ready!

DRIED SPAGHETTI SAUCE

At Home:

To dry homemade or commercial spaghetti sauce, strain the sauce through a large-holed colander to separate out any large chunks to dry on their own.

Lightly oil a leather sheet and spoon on the sauce, smooth out, and dry until the spaghetti sauce will peel off the sheet. Dry at 110 to 135 degrees. Store in a self-sealing plastic bag.

In Camp:

Break the dried spaghetti sauce into one-inch pieces, cover with water, let sit, stir occasionally with a fork, adding more water if necessary. Jazz up the sauce by adding dried peppers, mushrooms, onions, tomatoes, and spices to the rehydrating sauce. When rehydrated, heat and serve over cooked pasta.

Once you've dried and rehydated spaghetti sauce, try drying split pea soup, refried beans, ketchup, cooked beans, and leftovers.

> The next time you wander the aisles of a health food store, check the price of dried split pea soup and note the texture. Then at home dry either a can of commercial split pea soup or your own homemade and rehydate to see how easy this really is.

THE ULTIMATE TRAIL MIX

W hat more could anyone want?—jerky, beer nuts, and pickles all in one! Drying pickles is really fun and easy. | Makes 6 cups.

• 2 cups jerky, cut in ½-inch pieces • 2 cups beer nuts, salted • 1 cup dried sweet or dill pickles, cut in ¼-inch pieces • 1 cup sunflower seeds, salted • 1 cup pumpkin seeds, raw • 1 cup dried coconut, shredded • ¼ cup sesame seeds, toasted

Slice or dice sweet or sour pickles in ½- to ¼-inch pieces, place on a mesh-lined dehydrator tray, and dry at 110 to 135 degrees until they are hard. Mix together all ingredients.

JUDY'S "WOW" HAM CURRY

I've witnessed many hungry hikers raving about this meal. | Makes 6 Servings.

At Home:

Remember to pack a whisk.

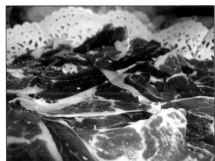

- 4 cups dried ham, ½-inch cubes
- 2 teaspoons dried minced onions
- 6 tablespoons flour • 2 teaspoons curry powder • ¼ teaspoon pepper • ½ teaspoon salt • 2 chicken bouillon cubes • 2 cups powdered milk • 8 ounces noodles • 1 cup Parmesan cheese • 6 tablespoons butter

In Camp:

Pour contents of bag #1 in a pan. Add 4 cups of water and let rehydrate at least 1 hour. Drain off and save excess liquid, adding enough water to make 4 cups. Use this water to boil and cook noodles. Remove from heat and cover.

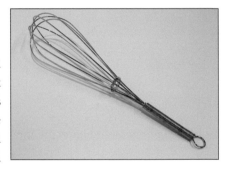

To make sauce, melt butter in a large pot. Add ingredients from bag #2. Add saved rehydration liquid and whisk until mixture thickens. Add contents of bag #3 and stir constantly while cooking over low heat. Combine sauce and noodles. Open bag #5 and sprinkle on top. Serve immediately.

To Package: • *Besure to number the bags.* • *Bag #1: dehydrated ham and dehydrated onion* • *Bag #2: flour, curry powder, pepper, salt, and bouillon* • *Bag #3: powdered milk* • *Bag #4: noodles* • *Bag #5: cheese* • *Put butter in plastic container*

VEGETABLE SOUP

The ingredients in this soup are dried separately and then combined with other ingredients that are rehydrated in camp. There's no limit to the variety of ingredients you can use in this soup: use dried ground meat or ground meat jerky, substitute noodles for potatoes, or change the seasonings. The meat is dried at 145 to 160 degrees on mesh-lined dehydrator trays. The vegetables are dried at 110 to 135 degrees on mesh-lined dehydrator trays until they are hard. | Makes 4 servings.

At Home:

Dry each of these items separately at home. The total weight of this soup when dried is 12 ounces.

• 1 pound meat strips, marinated • 2 cups blanched potatoes, sliced ¼-inch thick • 1 cup fresh zucchini, sliced ¼-inch thick • 2 fresh medium-size tomatoes, sliced ¼-inch thick • 1 cup fresh onion pieces, ¼-inch cubes • 1 cup fresh mushroom, sliced ¼-inch thick • ¾ cup fresh blanched green beans, ½-inch pieces • ½ cup fresh bell peppers, ¼-inch pieces • ½ cup fresh carrots, shredded • 2 tablespoons fresh basil

Once the above items are dry, put them in a one-gallon self-sealing plastic bag and add the following ingredients:

• 1 teaspoon salt • ½ teaspoon dried garlic • ¼ teaspoon powdered dried sage
• ¼ teaspoon black pepper • 1 bay leaf

In Camp:

Heat 3 cups water and add soup ingredients. Cover pan, remove from heat, and let rehydrate at least 1 hour. Larger pieces may take longer to rehydrate. Add more water if necessary and cook until all the vegetables are soft. Remove bay leaf before serving.

COOKED GROUND MEAT

This method of drying ground meat is popular with outdoor adventurers who want to add a lightweight high-protein ingredient to spaghetti sauce, rice, tacos, and other dishes. | One pound of fresh ground meat will dry to 5 ounces and will measure 1 ⅓ cup.

• 1 pound ground meat • 2 tablespoons onion, finely chopped • 1 tablespoon bell pepper, finely chopped • 1 tablespoon Worcestershire sauce • 1 teaspoon garlic, minced • ½ teaspoon dried basil • ¼ teaspoon black pepper, ground • 1 tablespoon oil

Sautee meat until browned. Press down on the pieces so they get as small as possible. Remove from heat. If there is a lot of fat, place the oily meat in a colander and spray with warm water to rinse oil off. Place in a bowl.

Sautee onions and peppers in oil until they become translucent. Remove from heat and add to the rinsed meat. Stir. Cool. Place on a leather sheet and dry until hard.

GOULASH

In this recipe you can use jerky or dried ground meat. | The total weight of this dried meal is 1 pound. Makes 6 servings.

At Home:

- 1 tablespoon olive oil • ½ cup fresh onion, cut in ¼-inch pieces • ¼ cup fresh pepper, cut in ¼-inch cubes • 1 teaspoon garlic, minced • 1 teaspoon dried basil • ¼ teaspoon salt • ⅛ teaspoon pepper
- 1 28-ounce can tomato chunks • 1 cup dried ground meat • 1 7-ounce package uncooked elbow macaroni

Put oil, onions, peppers, and garlic in a pan and sauté until browned. Add seasonings. Stir. Add tomatoes and cook until most of the liquid has evaporated. Cool, then spread the mixture on lightly oiled leather sheets and dry thoroughly. Dry at 110 to 135 degrees. Cool and tear dried goulash into 1-inch pieces.

In Camp:

In a pot, heat 2 cups of water to a boil and add contents of bag #1. Stir. Cover and let rehydrate at least 30 minutes. In another pot, boil 2 cups water, add macaroni from bag #2, bring to a rolling boil, and stir. Remove from heat, cover, and let sit 15 minutes. Covering saves cooking fuel. Stir the ingredients in both pots at least once. When the goulash mixture has rehydrated add the cooked noodles.

> To Package: Bag #1: dried goulash and dried ground meal; Bag #2: macaroni

DRYING HERBS

ADELINE'S SUMMER SAVORY CHICKEN

MINT CANDY

FLOWERS

POTPOURRI

WREATHS

CREATIVE DOUGH

PAPER

HEAVENLY CAT TOY

Herbs, Flowers, and Crafts

Drying Herbs

Plain and simple, drying herbs is easy! Knowing if the herb has either a small or a large internal stem is all you really need to know to be consistently successful.

Internal stems of large leafed herbs, like basil and sage, hold their moisture. After removing the leaf from the external main stem of a large leafed herb, the internal stem must be cut in half so that dry air can get inside. This will decrease the drying time and result in better color and flavor in the dried herb.

Herbs with small internal stems, like parsley, are stripped off the stem branch, the leaves are left whole, and they are laid on a mesh-lined dehydrator tray and dried at a temperature of 100 to 110 degrees until they are crushable.

To prepare for drying, herbs should be clean. Wash herbs in cool water and give them a spin in a salad spinner, gently pat with paper towel, or shake firmly to remove any excess water.

Herbs dry best between 100 to 110 degrees and most dry in a couple hours. All herbs need to be dried until they are crushable. Label containers with the herb name and drying date because dried herbs can be difficult to distinguish from one another. My favorite storage containers are recycled canning jars (dark ones are the best). Make sure the jars are completely dry.

To dry tiny herbs, like thyme, place a mesh sheet on top of a leather sheet. This will help prevent small herbs from falling through the dehydrator trays and onto the trays below. If the herbs are extremely lightweight and you need to stop them from flying around inside your dehydrator, lay another mesh sheet on top of the drying herbs to help keep them in place.

Let opportunity guide you throughout the growing season. As new, young plants appear, pick, clean, and dry them. We make a delicious and healthy tea out of dried young nettles, red clover, and red raspberry leaves. Drying herbs is one of the easiest and most rewarding things to do with a dehydrator.

Our drying season in the Midwest begins when the snow starts to melt and vibrant green watercress appears in our crisp, cold freshwater streams. We pluck the leaves from the stems, wash the watercress in cold water with a splash of vinegar, spin the watercress in a salad spinner, and dry. Throughout the year, especially during the dark days of January, dried watercress adds zing to our fresh fruit salads and baked potatoes.

ADELINE'S SUMMER SAVORY CHICKEN

Adeline, my mother-in-law, is a fantastic cook. Throughout the years, she's been a wonderful friend and a great help in contributing recipes to my books. This is her favorite dried summer savory chicken recipe.

- 1 chicken, cut in 6 to 8 pieces • 8 cups water • 1 tablespoon salt • 1 cup parsley, finely chopped • 2 teaspoons dried summer savory, crushed • 1 teaspoon black pepper
- 1 tablespoon (1 package) unflavored Knox Gelatine • ¼ cup cold water

Boil chicken, water, and salt for 2 hours in a covered pot. Remove from heat. Strain. Save 1 ½ cups of broth, avoiding the oil. Let chicken cool and pull it off the bone in strips with the grain. Put chicken in a bowl with parsley, savory, and pepper. Dissolve gelatine in cold water. Put the reserved broth in a pan and heat.

Remove from the heat and add dissolved gelatine, stir, and pour over the chicken mixture. Place in a glass bread pan. Press mixture down firmly with your hands until the liquid comes to the surface. Cover with Saran Wrap and refrigerate overnight. Slice ¼ inch thick.

Serve as an appetizer on crackers.

Crafts

Want to tap your creative energy by using environmentally sensitive ingredients to make imaginative and totally unique gifts? The dehydrator provides a way to make lovely personal gifts such as fruit and vegetable wreaths, cookie-like ornaments, homemade paper, and unlimited combinations of dried herbs and flowers for potpourris and sachets. You can also add dried herbs and flowers to homemade candles and soap.

Believe it or not, one time I made a baseball cap out of dried applesauce and jerky. Why, you ask, would anyone make a hat out of apple-sauce and jerky? Well, at the time I was busy teaching a food drying class and at the end of the class I decided to show the creative potential for using a dehydrator. I thought if I made an edible hat I could end the class with a big laugh. It worked, at least until our dog found it. Our dog also found my dried meatball, dried olive, and dried tomato necklaces and thought they were all special treats.

Mint Candy

In addition to using mint leaves to make candy, consider just about any herb leaves and edible flower to make exotic melt-in-your-mouth sweet treats. Dip clean petals or leaves in beaten egg white, sprinkle with confectioners' sugar, and dry on mesh-lined dehydrator trays at 100 to 110 degrees until they are crisp. That's it! Then eat these fancy treats or use them to decorate a bowl of ice cream or arrange on top of a cupcake.

Flowers

The method I choose to dry flowers is based on how I plan to use the dried products. Do I want color? Do I want aromatic flowers? Will the dried flowers and leaves be fillers or the main attraction in sachets and potpourris? Unlike most food drying advocates who dry only fresh, fragrant flowers, I also dry spent flowers. I just do not have the heart to dismantle a lovely arrangement until I have had time to enjoy it, and flowers, just past their prime, work well as fillers.

> Dehydrators dry flowers quickly, producing incredible colors and aromas. If you want to dry flowers, stem and all, a square or rectangular dehydrator works better than a round dehydrator because you can remove the shelves and create a larger drying chamber.

Throughout the growing season I dry whole flowers. Sometimes I break them apart into petals and leaves. I dry flowers until they are crisp, like corn flakes, and store them in recycled dark jars. When I have an ample supply, I combine them in creative and unique ways.

In addition to garden flowers, don't overlook drying wild and prairie flowers. I love how dried clover separates into tiny little trumpets and how Black-Eyed Susans and mums break up into colorful strands and round heads. Dry rose petals, rose buds, lavender blossoms, scented geraniums, dandelions, nasturtiums, chive flower heads, and yarrow, just to name a few. Let creativity be your guide.

Potpourris generally have a main scent, any number and combination of fillers, an essential oil, and a fixative, like orrisroot, is used. The main scent is the focus of the potpourri. Fillers are just about any combination of dried flowers, dried herbs, spices, berries, grains, root pieces, even wood chips and bark. Essential oils add fragrance, with rose and lavender being the most popular. A fixative is used to help hold the fragrance. Orrisroot, which is available in florist shops, is the most commonly used.

POTPOURRI

Feel the freedom to combine just about any dried flowers, dried herbs, spices, and essential oils to make your own personal blend.

• 2 cups dried flowers, any combination • 1 cup dried herbs, any combination • 2 tablespoons dried lemon peel, chunks • 2 tablespoons dried orange peel, chunks • 1 tablespoon orrisroot • 1 tablespoon ground spices, any combination • 1 tablespoon salt • 5 drops essential oil, your choice

Combine all ingredients in a large bowl and mix. Put in a decorative jar. Periodically add more essential oil as aromas fade.

Wreaths

Oftentimes culinary catalogs and home decorating magazines showcase gorgeous wreaths that have vivid combinations of dried fruits and vegetables, colorful fall leaves, pinecones, berry vines, whole spices, and decorative bows.

Linda Hazel is a local shop owner who is one of those people who can heat up her glue gun, attach just about any dried item to a wreath form, and end up with an attractive and inexpensive wreath. This wreath is one of her creations.

Dried food slices destined for wreaths are not intended to be eaten and last longer and get less discolored when infused with natural preservatives by soaking in a salt and vinegar solution.

Sleeping Pillow *Select a square of pretty fabric or use a fancy linen handkerchief and turn it into a three-sided pocket. Then fill it with various combinations of dried chamomile, rosemary leaves, pine needles, lavender flowers, sweet marjoram, and aniseed. Sew the end shut, trim it with lace, ruffles, and ribbons and you have a little scented pillow that can lie smoothly inside your pillowcase.*

You can dry sliced red, yellow, and green apples with or without the skins, unpeeled orange and lemons, peeled kiwi slices, and any hard vegetables, like squash, beets, and rutabaga.

Dipping Solution

To make food slices more colorful, add a few drops of food coloring to the dipping solution.

- $^2/_3$ cup vinegar • $^1/_3$ cup salt • Food coloring (optional)

Mix vinegar and salt together. Stir and add fruit and/or vegetable slices. Let soak at least 15 minutes. Place on a mesh-lined dehydrator tray and dry at 135 degrees until the slices are hard. Once dry, cover with hair spray to keep the slices from absorbing humidity from the air.

Ornaments

Lay a slice of dried food flat on a hard surface, then loop a ribbon around the top of the slices and use a glue gun to attach the ribbon to the dried slices. Decorate by gluing sprigs of rosemary, pinecones, cinnamon sticks, or star anise onto the dried slices. Hang up or use to decorate packages.

> **To make a wreath you'll need:** • *1 grapevine wreath form* • *Dried leaves* • *Hot glue gun* • *Dried fruit and vegetable slices* • *Ribbon*
>
> *Make a background base of the dried leaves, then glue on the food slices and decorate with a colorful ribbon.*

CREATIVE DOUGH

With artistic flair and various shapes of cookie cutters, turn dough into an assortment of ornaments. Shape, dry, and paint any design (stars, stripes, dots, geometric shapes), and then dry again.

• 1 cup flour • 1 cup water • 2 teaspoons cream of tartar • 1 teaspoon salt • 1 tablespoon vegetable oil • ¼ cup white glue • 15 drops food coloring (optional) • Hole punch

Mix flour and water together. Add cream of tartar, salt and oil. Stir. Add glue. You may want to put plastic gloves on to work the dough into a smooth mixture, or keep your hands wet enough so the dough does not stick to you. Divide the dough into thirds and mix different food colorings into each third until well blended. On a floured cutting board, roll dough out as thin as possible with a floured rolling pin. Be creative in combining colors to make designs. Keep  surface dry with enough flour. Spray the inside of the cookie cutters with oil so the dough will not stick when pressing down to make various shapes. When taking cookie cutters off the dough, use the side of the knife to keep the edges clean. With a small hole punch, make a hole in the top of the ornament in order to hang it. Then dry at 130 degrees until hard.

Paper

Paper, as we know it today, originated in China. People shredded the bark of mulberry trees, mixed it with scraps of linen and hemp, saturated it with water, and then beat it into a pulpy mixture. A mold was dipped into the

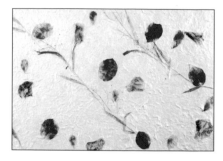

wet pulp to form a sheet of paper. The wet paper was placed in a sunny spot to dry. Today, paper is generally made in paper mills, where wood pulp is mixed with water, forming a slurry which is spread onto screens, dried, and pressed.

Because the job of a dehydrator is the removal of water, it is the perfect tool to make paper from a variety of sources. My favorite fiber is leftover pulp from juicing fruits and vegetables. These fibrous foods offer wonderful colors and textures. Carrots produce an orange fiber, apples make yellow, green, and brown, beets yield magenta, broccoli provides green, radishes pink, corn is a terrific yellow and long-fibered pulp, and celery and okra are also excellent choices.

Along with the leftover juice pulp you can add dry pulp paper, which is available in craft supply stores. You can make fiber by tearing paper towel, bathroom tissue, or newspaper apart. Soak paper shreds in water until they become soft and mushy and place in a blender, adding only enough water to blend thoroughly.

You'll need a rolling pin, a 6-inch square sponge at least ½-inch thick, 2 mesh screens, and waxed paper. Slurries can be formed into any shape.

1 cup dry paper pulp
1 cup water
1 cup leftover fruit or vegetable pulp

Combine all ingredients in a blender until the slurry is well mixed. Lay a dry sponge down on a large cutting board and place a mesh screen on it. Spread the slurry on top of the mesh and press down firmly with a spatula or your fingers. Push the slurry into the desired shape—hearts, circles, triangles, half moons, cones. To keep the slurry as thin as possible, place a second mesh sheet on top of the slurry, lay the wax paper on the mesh sheet, and use a rolling pin to push the water into the sponge. This will help make the paper a consistent thickness. Blotting out the extra water will force the fibers to bond with each other and to hold together. Carefully lift the mesh sheet straight up and place the paper on a mesh-lined drying tray.

Dry at 130 degrees until dry to the touch. When dry, gently bend the mesh sheet and remove the dried paper. Finally, paint your paper creations.

Papermaking can be an easy and rewarding classroom project that teaches recycling, as well as an appreciation for the paper we use and toss away.

Variations *While the slurry is still wet, press dried asparagus fern leaves, flower petals, lavender, rose, or marigolds petals into it.*

Heavenly Cat Toy

• Firm fabric • Yarn • Felt • Cotton balls • 1 tablespoon dried catnip • Embroidery floss

Cut out a fabric base. Fold the fabric with right sides together and cut out two oblong bodies to create a mouse. Cut two ears from felt. Braid yarn and knot the end to form a 2 ½-inch tail. Place the two body sections with right sides together and sew a ¼-inch top seam from A to B. Clip curves. Pin tail to base at point B, extending tail inward. Pin right side of body to right side of base, matching points A and B on base and body pieces. Sew from the middle of one side to nose. Leave needle in fabric and pivot to form point. Continue sewing around body and past tail. Leave a 1 ½-inch opening. Trim seam (especially at nose). Turn mouse right side out. Using a needle, gently pull the nose all the way out. Stuff two cotton balls in the nose and head. Add catnip. Continue stuffing with cotton until firm. Sew opening together by hand. Fold base of ears together and hand sew to each side of head. With embroidery floss make eyes (French knots), nose (a few straight stitches), and whiskers (knot thread 1 inch from end, run needle through nose, knot other side, and clip 1 inch from knot). Give to your cat as a special gift.

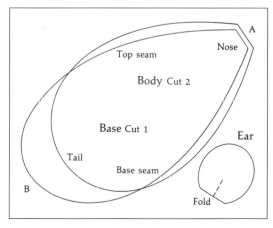

GROUND MEAT DOG TREAT

GROUND MEAT CAT TREAT

GUS'S FAVORITE TREAT

BIRD TREATS

BIRD SEED WREATH • BIRD SEED COOKIES

Pet Treats

Dogs and cats can be our best friends, our children, and our surrogate mates. We have two German Shepherds and we do our best to feed our four-legged family members good food, including special dried treats.

There is a huge difference between commercial dried cat and dog treats and what you can easily and inexpensively make yourself. Most commercial treats are baked, like cookies. They contain a minimum amount of protein and maximum amount of fillers, generally in the form of grains (rice, corn, wheat, and soy), along with artificial colorings, preservatives, salt and "by-products." In fact, the labels will tell you that some treats contain no protein whatsoever. Home-dried treats are dried at a low temperature in contrast to the high temperatures used in baking, and therefore are considered a more "raw" food.

By making your own natural, healthy, high protein pet treats, you can select each ingredient and address each pet's particular needs. Does your pet refuse to take its medicine? Does it have allergies or food sensitivities? Do you have a finicky eater, an older pal with dull teeth, or a buddy that's under the weather? Would you like to eliminate chemicals, artificial colors, and preserva-

tives from your pet's diet and have them eat healthier and more natural food? Would you like to make a thoughtful gift for a friend's special friend?

Cats are carnivores and they want meat. They love dried fish, calamari, shrimp, chicken, and turkey. Dogs are omnivores and can survive on plants, but they really enjoy beef, bison, lamb, turkey, and chicken. Dogs should not have chocolate, onions, raisins, grapes, or macadamia nuts. Avoid adding yeast, minimize dairy products, and keep garlic and salt to a minimum.

They love liver, which turns a shiny, dark brown color when dried. When drying liver, select fresh liver because frozen turns to mush when thawed.

Option #1

Dry unflavored strips or plain ground meat. Cut beef, bison, turkey, or chicken breasts and liver in $\frac{1}{8}$- to $\frac{1}{4}$-inch narrow strips. Place on mesh-lined dehydrator trays at 155 degrees until hard. Or grind any meat, flatten or shape it, and place on a leather sheet to dry.

> **A Good Idea** *Set your dehydrator outside when drying liver—it will generate a very strong smell that dogs love, but humans don't.*

Option #2

Grind flavored or unflavored meats and dry on leather sheets at 155 degrees. When dry, sprinkle on your pet's regular food. Cats like small pieces. Dogs don't care. Generally three pounds of fresh ground meat dries to about 1 pound.

Cat portion	— ½ to 1 teaspoon
Small dog	— 1 teaspoon
Medium-size dog	— 1 tablespoon
Large dog	— 2 tablespoons

Option #3

Marinate strips and flavor ground meat.

Dog Strip Marinade • 1 pound liver strips, cut ½-inch thick, 1 inch wide, and 5 inches long • ¼ cup soy sauce • 1 tablespoon honey • 1 teaspoon olive oil

Mix ingredients and marinate strips at least 3 hours, drain, then dry at 155 degrees until hard.

PLAY TIME

Use cookie cutters or a jerky gun to shape ground meat pet treats. Make your dog homemade "bones" and your cat some fish-shaped goodies. Spray the inside of the cookie cutters with oil so the mixture will not stick. Place cutters on oiled leather sheets. Spoon a small amount of meat mixture into the cookie cutter. Use the end of a spoon to push the mixture into the shape. The treats should be ¼- to ½-inch thick. Leave the cookie cutter in place on the dehydrator and dry until you can pull the cookie cutter away from the shape. Dry at 155 degrees. When you can pull off the cookie cutter, place the pet treat cookie on a mesh-lined dehydrator tray. This will allow dry air to get to it more easily. When checking for doneness, make sure the center is completely dry.

Cat Strip Marinade *Anchovy extract is available in most grocery stores.*

1 pound chicken strips, cut ¼-inch thick and in 1-inch cubes • ¼ cup anchovy extract • 1 teaspoon turmeric, ground • 1 teaspoon olive oil

Mix ingredients and marinate strips at least 3 hours, drain, then dry on mesh-lined dehydrator trays at 155 degrees.

GROUND MEAT DOG TREAT

These treats make great training rewards.

- ½ cup rice, cooked • ½ cup chicken broth • 2 tablespoons dried kale, crushed
- 1 pound fresh ground beef • ½ cup dried Parmesan cheese

Mix rice, broth, and kale together. Add meat and cheese and mix thoroughly. Let sit at least 1 hour and then shape. Place on mesh-lined dehydrator trays and dry at 155 degrees until hard.

GROUND MEAT CAT TREAT

Turmeric makes a yellow treat and dried pulverized beet powder is a natural way to get a red treat. | This makes 3 cups of ½-inch treats.

- 1 pound fresh ground turkey • ½ cup powdered milk • ¼ cup dried ground liver • ¼ cup chicken broth • 1 teaspoon turmeric

Mix all ingredients thoroughly. Let sit at least 1 hour and then spread evenly on heavily oiled leather sheets. Dry at 155 degrees. When dry, cut into ½-inch pieces.

Option #4

Gus, our German shepherd, is a finicky eater. He would take a piece of food out of his bowl, walk around, finally eat it, go back, look at his bowl, take another piece, and wander around the house. Meanwhile, his mom, Queen Ali, would wait until Gus got far enough from his bowl to grab some of his food. Over the years Ali got fat and Gus stayed too thin. Finally, one day we mixed this treat in with Gus's food and for the very first time, he finished his entire bowl of food without wandering away.

GUS'S FAVORITE TREAT

This treat uses already dried meat. Mint is added to serve as a breath freshener. | This makes 84 teaspoon-sized pieces.

- ½ cup ground dried turkey breast • ½ cup ground dried ground liver • 1 cup chicken broth • ½ cup cooked rice • ¼ cup carrots, shredded • 2 tablespoons oil
- 2 tablespoons cornmeal • 1 teaspoon dried mint, crushed

In a bowl, combine turkey, liver, and chicken broth. Stir and let rehydrate 3 hours. Add remaining ingredients. Put in a blender and grind, adding a little water when necessary. Scoop a teaspoon at a time and place on a heavily oiled leather sheet, flatten, and dry at 155 degrees until hard.

Option #5

Stephanie Marcous, owner of Grrrmet pet food company in Arlington, Washington, has her own high-end dog and cat pet treat line. One of her specialties is Puff Balls that are made with chicken, beef, and lamb that are ground to the chunky stage.

- ½ cup dried ground beef, crumbled • ½ cup chicken broth • ½ cup rice, cooked
- ¼ cup carrots, grated • 1 tablespoon powdered milk • ½ teaspoon salt

Mix ingredients together, shape, and then dry at 155 degrees on leather sheets.

Option #6

Easy Treat

Open both ends of a can of dog or cat food. Run knife around the inside of the can several times to loosen the food. Push the food out on to a cutting board. Slice into ½- to ¼-inch rounds, cut in half, and then cut in half again. Place on a mesh-lined dehydrator tray. If very juicy, lay the mesh sheet on top of a leather sheet, and then when half dry, remove the leather sheet so air can more easily get to all surfaces and dry completely. Dry at 155 degrees until hard.

Bird Treats

It's true—drying is for the birds! Tempt wild birds to come closer by offering enticing goodies. Birds love little pieces of dried peppers, broccoli, carrots, and beets. Birds are no strangers to eating dried stuff, since most of the year it is the basis of their diet.

> **A Sweet Memory** *My first garden is one of my most treasured childhood memories. My Dad and I always gardened together, and when I was nine, he gave me my very own tilled and ready-to-plant section. He said I could plant whatever I wanted. I chose sunflowers. It became a sunflower forest, and I loved sitting under those big leaves and mammoth heads. In fall, Dad and I harvested the seeds, dried them on old window screens, and together we fed the birds through the winter.*

BIRD SEED WREATH

This is a project that will bring joy to the giver and sustenance to the receiver. Using a large hook, hang this wreath outside where you can watch the birds. Remember to bring it inside before it rains. | Note that a 1-pound package of frozen vegetables will dry to 1 cup.

- 2 ½ cups applesauce • 2 ½ cups mixed birdseed
- 1 cup frozen mixed vegetables, dried

Combine ingredients in a bowl. Rub enough oil on a round leather sheet to completely cover it. Place the oiled sheet inside a dehydrator tray. Spoon half of the mixture on the leather sheet and press down firmly and flatten with your hands. Lay a round mesh sheet on top of the mixture and push it down firmly. Spread the other half of the birdseed mixture on top of the mesh sheet and flatten with your hands. Place in the dehydrator and dry at 135 degrees until it holds together. Take the filled mesh sheet off the leather sheet, turn over, and dry until hard. Remove. Push a shower hook through the birdseed coated mesh sheet. Hang outside and watch the birds feast. When the birds have stripped the mesh sheet clean, start the process over again.

Bird Seed Cookies

Use the same ingredients as the birdseed wreath along with various cookie cutters to make shapes so your bird can eat a cat, or your dog can snack on an elephant. Heavily spray the inside of the cookie cutters with oil. Place the open cookie cutter on an oiled leather sheet in a dehydrator tray. Fill the cookie cutter and press the mixture down firmly. Dry at 135 degrees until the birdseed cookie can be turned over and the cookie cutter can be lifted off. Then dry the cookies until they are hard on both sides. With a needle and heavy thread, poke a hole and push the thread through so these cookies can be hung.

Index